In a Square
Triangle

S. AMINAH NIALIAH

PAGE PUBLISHING, INC.
New York, NY

First originally published by Page Publishing, Inc. 2019

ISBN 978-1-64462-807-2 (Paperback)
ISBN 978-1-64462-808-9 (Digital)

Printed in the United States of America

Volume 1

FOREWORD

To begin, I want to say, Mariea could not be just plain or ordinary. There was no way she was living between two very different worlds. She actually lived between heaven and hell.

Independently, she survived. She went to work at age twelve, while perpetrating a thirteen-year-old. She had the paperwork to prove it. She worked on tobacco beside all those grown women. She pulled her own weight. She got up at 4:00 a.m. to catch the bus. She took a can of tuna fish and made six sandwiches for her daily meals. There was a bag of apples for her daily desserts along with penny candies. They were mostly Bit-O-Honey candies. She drank fountain water to fill in the gaps. She slept going to and coming from work on the bus. She bathed and ate dinner. She then did her chores and she went to bed when the sun went down. Dead tired, she set her alarm.

She took cooking and sewing from the fourth grade through high school. She acquired a Singer sewing machine from a friend's mother who no longer needed it. So what clothing her biological dad didn't buy for her, she made for herself.

She compensated very well, for her family's shortcomings. No one cleaned, cooked except (her mother), sewed for her, or paid her way. Yet she thrived, even survived on an upper level. She was short, dark-skinned, and nappy-headed. Yet she thought, she was just a cut above.

For deep down inside, she knew she was not average, but this was what she was supposed to do. She was of the age to help her family where it was needed.

Survival from an early age in life on a certain level was absolutely a necessity. This was to get her to wherever this life would take her.

All that was because being where she was just would not do. So she fought to overcome here circumstances. Therefore, she never wanted to settle for mediocre.

She saw the rainbows with all the colors, but getting to her pots of gold, through the muck and mess, is where the strength of excellence came in and purpose was achieved for her through God's perfect will for her life.

INTRODUCTION

In my push for excellence, my everyday life was actually between heaven and hell.

Mariea was one of ten children, the oldest. There were four different sets of families.

Her father's children consisted of, two girls, two boys and her. There was another sister and brother from her father, separate from his household. She had her mother's children, one girl, two boys, and her, one of which died at age three. There were two adopted brothers raised in her mother's house as well. There were, in spite of all odds, no circumstances insurmountable enough to keep their lives from intertwining. She had a tough job being a girl.

She had to set an example for the boys. This was not so tough when it came to the girls. However, supervision on a daily basis in the hearts of the ghettos of Connecticut and New York, with the toughest of the tough, made her always aware of her surroundings.

Something on that vein, she gave to them all.

However, they all realized their scars from the experiences of their daily lives.

S. Aminiah Nialiah, also known as Saundra Foster
Faithful one who is trustworthy

CHAPTER 1

Back in the 1800s, there was a freed African who went by the name of Black Jack. He jumped the broom with a Cherokee bride/wife. The two of them had several sons and daughters together. Those two were Mariea's great-grandparents.

One of his sons was named Frank, born in February, 1890. Frank married Olivia. Those were Mariea's grandparents. They had thirteen children (eight sons and five daughters). Frank worked and retired from the railroad in the Southern Hills of Georgia.

Picture that.

So they had courage, energies, ambition, and *a lot* of love. It had to be love with thirteen children. They decided to migrate up North with all thirteen of them.

Now, Mariea's grandparents were churchgoing people. They were God-fearing people. They were kind people who found their way up north from the deep Down South.

Mariea's grandparents migrated up north from those southern hills of Georgia. Frank's sons went first. A few of them went at a time. With so much courage, her uncles went to Connecticut. One stopped and stayed in New York. He was different. I don't know what he did, but it wasn't picking fruit or tobacco like the others. The others went to Connecticut and farther North to New Hampshire. They all worked, tobacco or at gardener's nursery, picking fruit. They were saving all their monies except for needed essentials. They had to make the way to go back to get their father. After saving even more money, they went back Down South. This time, it was to retrieve her grandma and their sisters. When the aunties arrived, they worked on tobacco or cleaned others houses.

All but one came, who at that time was on the chain gang because she had a child by the man she worked for. The wife of that man pressed charges.

She came later and opened up a restaurant/bar and did very well.

They all found living up north was far different from living in the South.

Yet they all thrived, found mates, and made families.

This family was close to one another. They always looked out for one another. Their mother or father never wanted for anything.

Though my grandfather did something that puzzled me. He would go to West Hartford and solicit by going door to door telling people about God. Now I guess you would associate him with the Jehovah's Witnesses, but at that time, Mariea could not understand it. She really couldn't understand why people would give him money.

He was a minister, Revered Frank. He saved enough money to open up a couple of storefront churches. He ended up owning Zion Apostolic Church of God. He preached the word of God in his church and at home.

We had other followers of God in our family.

I guess, we all believed. Yet most of us are worldly.

CHAPTER 2

Mariea's granddad had a temper, but we never took that serious. What we did take serious was his mean thump on your head. He didn't need a belt to reprimand you.

He would tell her stories of the Railroad, the South, and Black Jack the African who was his father. He told her all about her great-granddad. He told her about his wife the Cherokee Indian. She was my great-grandma. Oh, how I loved to sit at his feet and listen to him talk about those times and the many places. He told real life stories about, the cotton picking in the South, the chain-gang, the dignity and morals of a family's code.

He could cook as well. He taught her how to boil hamburgers. He also made apple turnovers from scratch which he taught me to do.

Now there was a milk machine on the complex where they lived. He would send her to the machine with a quarter for milk and a nickel for her. She loved to eat, but she never liked milk not even as a baby. Yet she was made by him to drink a glass of milk before her meals.

Oh, how I love Jesus, oh how I love Jesus, because he first loved me.

Mariea's grandmother was the sweetest, soft-spoken woman on earth. She was full of wisdom and kind words.

She loved to go fishing. Mariea and her grandma would dig worms on Friday. So most Saturday mornings, they would be brought by one or another of her uncles to a fish bank. Mariea learned to bait her own hook in time and she caught many fish. They would come home to her grandparents' house to clean and fry fish.

She always cooked hot breakfast on Sundays. She would cook biscuits, grits, sausage, or bacon or fatback, all before they went off to church. They would eat their breakfast and arrive at church on time.

She made pear and grape preserves from scratch and Mariea would help. She would store some preserves for the winter and give family members the others. She also taught Mariea how to prepare hog's head cheese. She showed her how to cook the parts, grind them up, and chill it until it molded.

Her grandmother washed clothing by hand until one of her sons delivered her a wringer-type washing machine. Her clothing that was hung on the line was so very white. It would make you wonder how she did it.

Mariea learned much about cooking and cleaning from her grandma. Mariea had the pleasure of spending part of her life with these two people. She loved those two people. They were good to her.

They were around long enough to help strengthen those of us that they left behind much too soon.

CHAPTER 3

Mariea's mom was the youngest of the five daughters. She had two brothers younger than she.

Mariea's mom, Lillie, dropped out of high school in the eleventh grade. This was after she had sewn a white classmate's finger with her sewing machine. This happened in her sewing class. That girl had called her out of her name.

Lillie got pregnant by her first love shortly after that.

She fell in love with Cal. He had been left in a field, by his mother. This was down in Florida. He was found by one of his uncles. He was brought from Southern Florida to Connecticut. He lived in Hartford with his grandmother who raised him. He went to Trinity College.

Shortly afterward, Lillie got pregnant. He was then forced to join the Air Force by his grandmother.

That appeared to be his penalty for committing that crime.

Just about the same time all this was happening, he learned that his dad whom he had never known, he learned that he had been shot down. This was in those same streets of Hartford, Connecticut, that he was now leaving to go to the Air Force.

This was Mariea's granddad, on her father's side of the family. He was shot in the back in the streets of Connecticut by a police officer.

He was just another police officer who got no time for the shooting her granddad in the back and killing him.

CHAPTER 4

Lillie was sent from Connecticut to live in New York. One of her brothers and a sister lived there now. This was where she was to give birth.

Now, I don't know that Mariea ever really thought that she aspired to be an actress. Yet she has been a performer for sixty, yes sixty, some odd years. No, I'm not going tell you sixty what, but she was born by the river. No, sir. No, sir. Picture this—Harlem, New York, in August 1950, hot bright lights, not a quiet night. There was stars, the heavens, the ambulance, and Sydenham Hospital. My mom and me. I was born there in Harlem in 1950. Me. Mariea.

That didn't last too long though. My grandparents thought we should not live in Harlem. So Hartford, Connecticut, here we come.

Her stay in New York at that time was brief because Lillie was getting wild in the streets of New York. Sometimes while going with her brother Frank Jr. to card games, she would have his back by carrying a gun. She was very familiar with the streets of New York night clubs and otherwise.

The word got back to her parents in Connecticut.

Lillie's dad Frank went to New York, and he brought the mother and daughter back to Connecticut. There was no need for discussion about the matter. He was the boss.

Mariea was now to grow up in Connecticut.

Times were hard for her in Hartford.

CHAPTER 5

So love brought Mariea to Hartford, Connecticut, and love sustained her through those early years of which she doesn't remember the first one or two of. But she started using her mind and her limbs at the age of three.

I said three, *huh*?

Now, how do I know that? You know how we carry stories down from the past? So I heard it over and over again how I showed my Uncle Frank how to get from my house to my grandmas. He was named Frank like my granddad. So I should say Frank Jr. They told how I look at him as he drove us in his car. We went from my mother's house down those streets of Hartford, to my grandma's house. I told him where to turn because I knew the way at three. I knew because I had walked it day in and day out with my mom. Bits and pieces of my mind set into place between ages four and seven.

I must understand by now that I live between heaven and hell.

It was either that fiery, inferno or that real very peaceful place.

I am five and it was first day of school, kindergarten. I remember that so well because my mom only walked with me on some days. I didn't think she should stop walking me to school.

I know, times then were not like they are now. So it was only five blocks straight with no main street to cross and no crossing guards. I thought it was far and I was scared.

This was the place where the library was on the corner that I needed to turn at to get to my house.

It was only my mom and me for a long time. Then I remember several men in our lives. They had cars and beer. I liked Ballantine beer with the three rings that looked like a pretzel in my mind. Yuck, good. I was permitted to drink some.

I loved my mom. She was good to me as well.

CHAPTER 6

I realized by the age of seven that a lot of things were starting to happen to me in my life.

My grandparents lived in a project called Nelton Court. This housing project was a different kind of project. There were white people there. Mariea had many white friends. One in particular named June.

Her grandparents had the first television in the neighborhood. They liked to watch baseball, the Yankees, soap operas, and Joe Frazier in his Friday night fights.

Mariea had a pair of roller skates at their house. She tore them up skating all the time. She knew not to ask for another pair. So she took the wheels off and put them on a piece of wood panel and she made a skateboard. She had seen one of her male cousins do this. She took the skateboard out one day when she was visiting her grandparents' house. She rode down the hill with it on Nelson Street. She rode right into Main Street traffic. Her skateboard was taken away from her for good.

My granddad chewed tobacco. One particular day, I found myself trudging up Nelson Street to the third store of the day. I was looking for Apple Tobacco with my nickel for pumpkin seeds.

When I finally reached the corner of Clark Street, I just ran across the street. I dropped my nickel in the middle of the street. I knew because I could see it. I also could see the car coming as I ran back to get it. Yet something in my mind told me, *It will stop*. But the car didn't stop for me. It hit me. I laid on the ground in the street only half knowing what was going on. I knew that I couldn't get up. I was finally taken to the hospital by an ambulance.

I had a concussion, sprained wrist, and multiple contusions. I spent eight days on the critical list.

I was conscious of the nurse. She kept asking, "What is your mother's name? Where does your mother work? What is your father's name? Where does your father work? What is a young girl, so little doing so far away from home?"

I finally could hear my mother's footsteps. After which, I was able to recognize all my visitors by their footsteps because I couldn't see very well with only one eye.

One of my aunts, Mary, came to see me. She showed me myself in the mirror. My left eye had a bandage on it. My face was all messed up. I cried.

I underwent many treatments, horrible treatments. There were so very many tests. They even put guck in my hair. They put wires in my hair. My hair was hard and napped up.

My family was ever so close. Yet my grandma never came.

My friend, Jimmie, in the bed next to me had a broken leg. So he couldn't go to the bathroom. I cried for him. I thought they had hurt him.

He went home too soon. The only real friend I had in the hospital.

Everyone was nice to me, but he was black like me.

I was left alone.

So this car accident made me wonder what I had done so bad that all this would happen to me.

They finally released me from the hospital. I was taken home to my grandma's house.

My mom has now washed my hair twice. It was still like wire. It hurt to comb and brush it. I cried. I had scars on my face and nappy, kinky hair.

I felt like I could never go back to school.

CHAPTER 7

I was always making new friends. Therefore, I hurt inside, I feared, and I prayed. I prayed, every day for myself.

Now, we were living in a rooming house, my mom, my uncle Walt, and me. This was the uncle I sang at church with.

This house had the cemetery in the back, right outside the bathroom window. So while bathing, I thought of the dead on the other side of the wall. There was no one out there that I knew so it didn't bother me much.

My mom started talking to a man named Jon while we lived there. This was one of the men who worked with my uncle Walt.

Now this man was nice. He had been eating dinners at my house on Sundays. That was starting to be very often.

This was all before I started peeking through the bedroom door's keyhole at him and my mom.

I told my so-called friends what I saw. They told my mom. She beat me good and punished me as well.

So I talk too much. I talk about things I know, things I see, and I learn the hard way. I got bloody noses and beatings. My mom didn't play.

She said, "You can think that you can do very well. However, you can't say all that is in your mind, you can't trust all who say they are your friends, nor can you ever talk family business to people outside the family."

So I learned the hard way that silence is golden.

CHAPTER 8

We moved shortly after that incidence. My mom got married. She got married to this man, Jon, who worked with my Uncle Walt.

Not too long after we moved, my mom had a baby. It was around Christmas. I remember because she wasn't around near Christmas. She came home just a day before with my baby sister. I was on school vacation for the holiday. She came and got me and took us home.

Really, this was happening, now. No more "just Mom to myself." Then I got one brother, then another brother.

Oh yeah, in the midst of all this, I had a maternal dad. So I had more sisters and brothers.

My dad came to visit me from time to time.

In our new apartment, we didn't live with my uncles. There were no uncles with us now. Just our family who lived there. We lived on Liberty Street. We lived on the top floor.

I remember having an iron which had a cord. Somehow, the cord became a loose. I thought I had taped it well. Therefore, I tried to plug it up, but fire shot out of the hole and my mom took it from me. I cried and my stepfather fixed it properly. Now I can continue to iron my doll clothes.

Other bad things happened to me one right after another.

One day, my girlfriend Linda, fell off the fence. She cut herself very badly. It seemed as though her fall was my fault. You see, we were both climbing over the fence. However, she got stuck on the fence. The only thing holding her was her pants and I couldn't help. I tried, but it didn't work. I could only watch her rip her leg straight down the side, scream, and bleed. I couldn't leave her not even to go to get help.

Finally, help came and she went to the hospital. She received a lot of stitches.

On another occasion, while we were living on Liberty Street. We decided to cross the railroad tracks to get to Barnard Brown School that day.

There were a few of my friends, Regina and me We were just getting onto the track to cross the railroad tracks. A train was coming. We could hear it blowing the horn. We started to run across. One of my friends, Regina, got her shoe caught when the tracks changed over for the oncoming train. She couldn't get her shoe off in time.

She got hit by the train. Actually, the train ran over her legs and chopped them right off. She didn't die, but she lost her legs. I didn't know what to do. So I went back home. I told my mom. My mom called the police and the ambulance came and took her to the hospital.

My mom scolded me about being on the tracks. After seeing that happen, I was never doing that again. Anyways, she remained in the hospital for a very long time. I remembered visiting her when she got home. It was sad to look at her with no legs. Yet I overcame that. We remained friends for life, even after we moved away from each other.

She was at peace with the fact of not having her legs. She was just glad to be alive.

CHAPTER 9

We now live on Winthrope Street. This was very close to Windsor Street which was a place where everything went on. There were all different kinds of people and all kinds of things happening on Windsor Street.

My stepfather Jon started to drink more. I don't know what really happened to him. I do know that he got his throat cut. He also had multiple chest wounds.

We thought he would die. He lived on to get walking pneumonia. He didn't work much now.

At this apartment we had a next-door neighbor. Our neighbor Ms. Jesse was a really nice lady. I ran errands for her. I got paid well.

My school was the same as before we moved. The rear entrance of Barnard Brown School that I attended was just across the street from our house. I attended a church which was also just across the street right next to the school. So I didn't have to walk far to get to school or church.

I was told by my mom that I was never to go to Windsor Street. However, they had everything there. They had candy apples and all kinds of stores. I could look into the windows and dream. The State Theatre was also on Windsor Street. That was the theatre where James Brown and Little Anthony and the Imperials appeared.

I could not resist taking the chance, once in a while, to go to Windsor Street. I found out that the people were really different. So I would stand in the alley for hours just looking. Yet you got wise quick. There were drunks and funny-looking and acting people who passed by me. They sometimes took notice of you. They said things to me and I knew then why I was out of place. I knew my mom said not to go there. I now surely knew why.

During the time we lived on Winthrope Street, I believed that some of my family members thought that we shouldn't live there. I think others in my family thought I was being mistreated.

I was in school one morning when I was sent to the dentist office. He checked my teeth. He said, "What happened to your tooth?"

I said, "It fell out."

He said, "Did your stepfather hit you in the mouth?"

"No, he doesn't hit me," I said.

Later to find out that a family member had notified the school authorities. They did think that I was being abused.

In this apartment, we had a kerosene burning stove. I had to go get kerosene for that stove. I carried the kerosene oil in a gallon glass jug. I went to the store down the street for it. Sometimes, I went in the early morning. Sometimes, I went in the dark of night. It got very cold when we didn't have it. So it had to be gotten.

At this apartment, we had a back porch. I used to stand on the back porch and watch the rats and mice run in the yard. I never, at that time, thought that they may be in the house as well.

CHAPTER 10

My dad still came around sometimes. He never left before he would take me shopping and buy my much-needed things.

My dad came once and he even took me to the State Theatre to see James Brown. He took both myself and a cousin who was staying over my house. I was in heaven. He promised to come to take me again at a later date and he did. This time, we saw Little Anthony and the Imperials. That's how I knew that stars appeared at the State Theatre on Windsor Street.

Not too long afterward, my mom told me that I was going to my dad's for summer vacation. I was delighted to know this.

The school year ended. I passed to the next grade. My dad came that weekend and took me to stay with him for my summer vacation. It seemed like that was a long time for me to be away from my mom. I was happy though.

They lived in a housing project called Charter Oak Terrace. My brothers and sisters loved my being around. We played many games. We loved each other. I was the eldest, I was kind to them, but I loved to tease them a lot. They didn't mind it though.

I found out that my dad played a trumpet. I really liked to listen to him play jazz which he did most evenings.

My stepmother Lo was a quiet-spoken woman. She sewed curtains and other fixings for the house. Later on in life, she taught me more sewing tactics. She added on to what I already knew and how to do from my school classes. She bathed me with tender loving care. She always washed my back.

My dad cooked most meals. His chili is still one of my favorites.

I was dismayed when it was time for me to leave them and go back home. Summer had gone by too fast. My dad took me shopping and bought me school clothes before bringing me back home to my mom.

My dad was an air records control person at Bradley Field Airport. His job got transferred to New York. So that part of my family life had to move to New York.

CHAPTER 11

We also moved again. We now lived on Bellevue Street. I now go to another school, Arsenal Annex, just down the street from where we now live.

There was a park across the street called St. Benedict. There was a center down the hill on Windsor Street that showed cartoons two nights a week. This was a very different part of Windsor Street. The things that went on in the other part of Windsor Street were not on this part of Windsor Street. Thank God.

This new apartment was worse than the last one was. I didn't like it at all, but who am I to say where we live.

I spent many nights, sometimes weeks with three of my aunts. Our family was large and they shared all of us kids. So it was nothing unusual, but I got to know my family very well.

I got to know the ones that were not in the church. Those were the ones that drank. I got to know the ones that are in the church. They too drank at one time or another. Some drank more than others and suffered for it. But they all had fun with each other.

There was a family living next door to us with the same last name. But they were not a part of our family. That was odd to me.

We had a lot of company now. My family of aunts and uncles were always there. They partied a lot.

Jon my stepfather worked off and on now. He didn't keep a job for very long at all.

That's when I realized there was a lot of fighting going on around me. The family members didn't fight with each other, but you didn't mess with any of them. They retaliated when someone did wrong one of them, verbally or physically. You soon found out that was not a good idea. My mom, her sisters, or brothers were not having it. They all fought men like they would fight a woman. So if you didn't want to fight, then you should not put your hands on them; they were not to be touched if it wasn't lovingly.

I learned that fighting was not a fair game. If you can reach it, use it. If you can't reach it, then use what you have. You can bite, poke in eyes, cut, and kick. All is fair game in love and war.

I remember on the day we were moving into that apartment. One of the men moving us in had too much to drink. He said something like "Out of the way" to one of us girls. My mom and my aunts jumped on the man. They beat him down. The police were called. I took the kids across the street. We watched them from across the street. My parents, my aunts, and my uncles all got put into the paddy wagon. They all went to jail.

One of my aunts told the police that she would stay with the children. We had already been sent to the park. We were still across the street. We were out of the police's sight. We were still watching. The aunt who said she was supposed to be watching us. She was up the stairs in the house in the window, laughing. The police went back upstairs. The police got her out of the window. They brought her down stairs. She went to jail as well.

We kids went into the St. Benedict's playground up the hill. We played a while before I took all the kids to our grandparents' house. We stayed there until we were retrieved by our parents. Our grandparents were angry. They fussed at our parents about the shame of their actions. So most of them took their children and went home. I got to stay with my grandparents for the night. I went home in the morning.

CHAPTER 12

I liked Arsenal Annex School. It was right down the street from my house. I made a few good friends. I was in the fourth grade and not having much trouble with my homework.

We didn't live too far from my grandparents. There was a grocery store next door to us and a drugstore on the corner. I was permitted to go to the park across the street. I could go to Windsor Street to see the movies once a week. I had a curfew. Never let darkness catch me outside my house.

I got into one fight at school, but it wasn't my fault. The other girl started it and I only used self-defense. I didn't get into too much trouble. The teacher sent a note home. My mom talked to me about it and dismissed it. I told her the truth.

We had a back porch at this apartment as well. In this house, like at the others, looking off the porch was no different. The rats and mice were all I saw looking out into the backyard from the back porch.

Not this again.

This apartment was different though. The rats or mice were now in my house at night. I had not noticed this until one night they were in our kitchen. I could almost hear them. They made our puppy bark. They were in other parts of the house as well.

In this apartment, my baby brother's crib was in my room. My baby brother started to cry. I got up and I turned on the light so I could calm him down and put him back to sleep. The mice were in the crib with my new baby brother. The light and my scream scared them away. It also awoke my mom.

I went back to bed with the light on. I didn't sleep anymore that night.

My mom took care of that the next morning. She decided it was again the right time to move. She set out looking for another apartment that day.

CHAPTER 13

She found an apartment in the projects that were not that far away. She explained our circumstances and we were able to get the apartment on an emergency status.

We moved into the Bellevue Square projects the next day. I think. I know it didn't take us too long to get out of that apartment after that night.

We moved into Bellevue Square during the time that they still had grass. This was before the asphalt came. By then, I must have been ten because I was in the fifth grade.

This place was much different from all the others. This new apartment seemed better. The buildings were close together. Most buildings were four flights up. There were many buildings just like this one. There were many families in one building. They had a whole project of these buildings with four floors. They had four or five families on each floor. They didn't have back porches, just yards all around the buildings.

They had a recreation hall and a playground. They had fenced-in clotheslines. Our apartment had a garbage space connected to it. So if you looked out of my bedroom window, you first saw the top roof of the incinerator as you looked out into the yard in the back of the house. I didn't see any of the rats or mice.

This was not like the project my grandparents lived in. Their apartments were one level. The apartments were connected side by side in a row. They faced the same structure across the yard. They all had outside clotheslines in their yards.

However, living in Bellevue Square was like living in a jungle. I soon noticed that there were many people: adults, children, dogs, and cats. At first, I was only allowed to play in the yard. I could sometimes go to the playground area after living there for a while.

This was fine, I was still getting myself accustomed to being there.

CHAPTER 14

Soon, I acquired playmates. There were many, many kids. Up until now, I had several close friends, but none to be as true or as totally false as these kids I now played around with were. Some of these kids had been only here. Other ones had been other places and hated it here.

I knew for us this was the best decision my mom could have made in our predicament. The rent was cheap. We didn't seem to have mice if there were any we didn't see them.

My stepfather still was not working for long periods of time. He still drank too much. We always had too much company. There was always a relative or friend of the families sleeping over. Never enough money in the house for many extras, but someone always had a bottle.

My mom always managed though. We would go over the bridge on Windsor Street to the park and pick Sallie Patches which were some kind of greens. They had a good taste. She cooked very good food. I used to sit in the kitchen and wait for the cornbread to come out of the oven. She would give me that first piece with some butter to eat before I went back outside.

I needed money for lunch now. Even though the school was right across the street from our house, we could not go home for lunch. So I needed money or I needed to bring my lunch. I ran errands for some of the elderly couples who lived in our building. I even took out some of the people's garbage.

This is when people started taking my kindness for a weakness. It was hard being me. These people who were fellow classmates wanted to know too much about who I was.

I was about four feet tall, really short. So my mom would let me take a rope to school to play with. This rope was long. So we could play double Dutch. Now, these girls were crazy. These chicks thought they could take my rope and play with it, but I couldn't play. So they tried their best to bully me. It is needless to say, I wasn't having it. I defended my property. I tried unsuccessfully to take my rope from them. This ended up with me fighting with the two who were turning. I used the middle of my rope to choke one of them. The other jumped on my back and I threw her off so hard she didn't retaliate.

I found myself in detention for fighting over my own rope. They didn't get to play with it again though.

I was new, but I was no pushover. I soon learned that they didn't want to be my friend. They just wanted what I had, especially my rope. Which, now I doubled up. I jumped with my own jumping rope alone.

CHAPTER 15

My fifth grade teacher was a very nice person. She seemed as though she cared about each and every one of us. She taught us a lot about how we should treat one another. She was just very good to us. She took us to her house for a picnic and fed us cookout style foods.

My sixth grade teacher was not so nice. My classmates were not so nice either. I didn't have many problems with my class work. However, I stayed in trouble with classmates and the teacher. I still fought often.

By now I had learned from my past experiences. I learned that being small like I was I had to try harder at everything. So I fought for my own identity.

Most of the girls' bodies were noticeably changing. Mine wasn't. So I got teased a lot for my shortcomings.

I stood up to boys as well as girls. I fought many boys and won. That meant that when the girls came at me, they sent their toughest. I fought gang leaders of the Spanish and blacks.

I started to have a lot of male friends. That was because most boys climbed trees. I became a fruit tree climber. I could not resist.

If I would pass a fruit tree in your yard, I would first look for your dog, then I would climb your fence, then your tree, pick your fruit, climb back over the fence, and then leave. I couldn't bring them home. I had to eat them, before I got there. I got so many whippings for climbing trees.

My mom would say, "I keep telling you, girl, you are not a boy and you need to stay out of them peoples' yards and trees."

Once, I had climbed to the top of an apple tree. I was struck in the eye by a rock thrown by someone below. I then fell off the tree, needless to say. By then, the tenants were alerted of my screams so we had to run out of their yard. We had to climb the fence. Not only did I have a black eye, but I also had smashed apples. I proceeded to get my pants caught on the fence. I had to rip them to get off the fence. I now had smashed apples and torn pants.

My mom was not pleased with me. She had no sympathy for my present condition. I had disobeyed her, and I was punished.

CHAPTER 16

I had to set a good example for my siblings. They thought I was tough since I always fought for them.

My mom thought I needed to severely change some of my ways. She didn't want my siblings to follow me down the road that I was traveling. She didn't think it would be safe for them. She tried to talk to me about mending my ways. She thought I should be more ladylike.

My sister was a good girl, quiet, and soft-spoken; she was really good and very obedient. My brother was not much to talk about. He threw rocks all the time and ran to me when someone bothered him. I guess that is what little boys did.

I was the chosen guardian. So I guarded them as we played, they played. My mother entrusted me with this duty. Therefore, I was never far away from them. I took this chore seriously. I loved them so very much. They never got hurt on my watch. I bathed them. I even cooked breakfast for them sometimes, or beans and franks for lunch. We all slept together.

I took care of them. I taught them how to survive in the jungle we lived in. The jungle that was inside and outside our house. That was one of my main duties.

There were always many people coming and going in my house. These people, both family and friends, played cards for money, and they drank.

CHAPTER 17

I asked my mom for the permission to accompany one of my friends to her dance class. I went with her to the dance class. I was hooked after watching them for the first time. I was sure that I could learn to do what they were doing.

I had one of my uncles, Uncle Dav, who tap-danced. So I kind of knew how; I just didn't know how to put it all together. We would trade eights. I didn't know what "eights" were at that time. But I was a young hoofer which amounted to him doing an eight-count step to eight bars of music, then I would do one back at him.

I asked my mom about the classes. I told her how much I enjoyed watching. She said that we couldn't afford it. She said that the girl I went with was white and can afford it.

I said, "So I am black. I don't know what the problem is. So the teacher of the dance school Phyllis Stone is white as well. I can dance better than my white friend can. I just don't smile." That was before I knew I had beautiful teeth.

I kept bothering my mom about the dance classes. She finally gave in to my begging her. She finally let me try the dance school. I volunteered to help pay Phyllis Stone for the classes. She permitted me to take the dance classes.

I couldn't afford new shoes for the tap class. I was allowed to purchase hand-me-down shoes from the studio. These were the shoes that others brought into the studio because they no longer fit them. This went on for years while I was struggling to pay for classes. I wore the shoes that the studio allowed me to take.

I stayed with my grandparents most of the weekends. My grandfather allowed me to earn money by going to the store for him and my grandmother.

I also shined shoes. One of my cousins took me with him downtown to shine shoes and he taught me how. Shoe shining didn't last too long. It was too slow-paced. I delivered groceries from our grocery store to the elderly. I delivered newspapers with one of the bigger kids in the community. He gave me a cut of his money he earned. I still take out garbage for other people. I tried to caddy, but I only lasted a few weekends.

Whenever I am given my lunch money, I hardly ever spent it on lunch. I ate big breakfasts, big dinners, and a piece of fruit and water for lunch.

I sometimes played cards with the people in my house. That was when one of my uncles was playing. I even beat them sometimes. My mom used to say, "In my father's house, we were not permitted to even have a deck of cards, much less to gamble."

Yet I was permitted.

I wanted to dance. I wanted to have the money to pay for it as well. I was serious about this dance class. I found peace in my dance. Peace no one could take away from me.

I really needed money now. I was taking two dance classes. I had gotten good. At the end of every class, our teacher would give us a new step and if you got it, you earned fifty cents. I always got it. That was absolutely necessary. This was so I could stop on the way home and get me a hamburger and fries.

I really loved that dancing school, but my first love was to dance. So I set myself about ways to make and to keep money.

CHAPTER 18

When I graduated from grammar school, they bought me a new dress and new shoes. Wow, I felt very special. I attended a graduation party not too far from where I lived. There were many of my school friends there. I enjoyed myself. It was wonderful.

I would be in the seventh grade at North East Junior High in the fall. This school was just on the other side of Nelton Court where my grandparents lived. So I could visit them on a daily basis.

For that summer, I went to work on tobacco. It was hard labor for a young twelve-year-old girl. I had the working papers to say I was thirteen. I got up at 4:00 a.m. to catch the bus right up the street from where I lived. It was on the corner of Main Street. I made it to the bus stop by 5:00 a.m. I worked hard all day in the sun. I made six sandwiches out of one can of tuna. To have two sandwiches for breakfast, two for lunch, and two on the way home to eat. I would buy five apples and penny candy to go with my sandwiches for the week. I drank fountain water on the job. I slept coming and going to work while I was on the bus. The money I made was a big help to me and my family.

On Friday, I would stop on the corner at the drugstore and cash my check. I would bring my check home. I would give my check to my mom. She would give me some of it. She would usually give me enough for my next week's lunch and a little more than pocket change. I spent wisely that summer. I opened a bank account, saved some of my money, and bought my lunch for the week.

One week, I worked with cardboard in my sneaker. I was counting on getting a new pair with that weeks' paycheck. However, I cashed my check. I took it home to my mom.

My mom said, "You did a good job. Would you go pay the house rent, please?" She said that I could get myself a new pair of sneakers next week. I now had to find a new cardboard box over the week end. This was to put into my sneaker to keep everything else out, allowing my foot to not get cut.

I felt as though, even though I never forgot that. I just figured this was what I was supposed to do. I was old enough to help and too tired of having to move. My family came first. It was survival of the fittest for me.

CHAPTER 19

At the end of the summer, I went to New York to shop for school. My dad took me shopping and let me keep some of the money that I had earned. He always bought me something. I took money back home with me and banked it.

I went to the seventh grade with a brand-new leather jacket, compliments of my dad.

I found that being in junior high school gave me great pleasure. The work was not too hard and I danced on Friday nights.

About this time, I got to go visit my family in New York on most weekends. I would leave after my dance class and I took the bus. I would get to Grand Central Station, call my dad, and take the subway. Sometimes someone picked me up. At other times, my brothers would meet me, and we would walk and talk. It was usually dark, but we were not afraid.

My dad now had another child. So I now had two brothers and two sisters there to enjoy. I slept in the room with my sisters. I played in the park across the street. I loved to play handball. They had the walls for it. I also ran the streets of New York with my brothers and my older sister.

My dad had a big house with three floors, and a basement that he rented out. He also owned another house. There was always a lot of company in my dad's house, but it was different. He had boarders. There were always people coming and going. Some of these people I knew, and others I hadn't seen before.

To me, he seemed like a godfather of sorts. He was always doing for other people. He was liked by both men and woman. He was smart though, he seems to be struggling. His struggle was not like my mother's though because he worked.

He had a good job. He worked at the airport. He worked as an air records control person full-time. They pay well, but he had a lot of obligations.

I loved going to New York. So I was allowed to visit on holidays and school closings. It is never long enough.

CHAPTER 20

A lot of other things happened during my junior high school years. My responsibilities were different. I would get up early to give me time to walk to Northeast Jr. High school from Bellevue Square.

I mentioned before when coming from home on my way to school I would stop in Nelton Court at my grandparents' house. My grandma would send me upstairs. She had a trunk in which among other things. She had nuts and fruit there. In that trunk she also had a nice, clean blouse. This blouse is for me to change into. It looks like it is new. How she gets white, so white. You can't touch this or me.

Then I would proceed on to school on time. I acquired so many skills along the way. This was while I was in the heaven, of my grandparents' house.

After school, I asked Mama, "Mama, can I spend the night?"

"No, it's a school night."

"Why?"

I went back to the hell that was my mother's house. It was hectic. Survival was everything.

I would always go to church on Sundays with my grandparents. This would be when I was not just returning from New York. That was when I would get to sing with my Uncle Walt. I would then be dropped off at home after church.

Most of my cousins would come over and it was my duty to take them to the movies. We would first stop next door to the Star Theater at the restaurant. We had money to eat the best hot dogs in town for lunch. Then we would proceed to go into the movies. I would get our tickets and popcorn. Then I would get our seats so we could watch the movie. After the movie, I would take them all back to my house. They would be picked up by their parents from there to go home.

CHAPTER 21

My baby brother was born with a heart murmur. He was three and he was sick. His heart was not functioning well. My other brother was now five, and my sister was seven. The both of them were adjusting to school very well.

Some white lady was visiting my house off and on. I found out that the people in school were asking my siblings questions. I started washing their clothing more often. I was fixing breakfast for them before I went to school. So now they were definitely clean and when asked what they ate, it was fresh on their minds. I talked to them and made them aware of what was going on.

The authorities could not make them turn against or lie on our mother. I let them know what was happening and why. Our mom was fit to be our mother, she just had some difficulties. That lady soon stopped coming around. No more questions were asked in school. I was smart enough to protect us in so many ways. I loved them so much and these people were not our family.

We still slept together. We prayed together, and we moved on together.

CHAPTER 22

My siblings and I had a big bed, so me and my siblings slept in the same room. I sometimes kept a stick or a knife close by while we slept. The door was always closed. I slept light.

However, some of our houseguests sometimes got lost. They would say that they were looking for the bathroom when they tried to enter our room. I had to let them know that they were not there. This was not it.

Our baby brother's crib was also in our room, so I usually hear him cry first when he wakes at night. I remember feeding him and letting him sleep in the bed with us. My baby brother got sick. My mom took him to the doctor. The doctor said that he must be put into the hospital for observation. He got better and came home.

My grandmother took his illness badly. His illness bothered her a lot. She loved him so much.

I guess during his hospital stay they diagnosed him with something that only open-heart surgery could fix. He already was not strong.

My grandmother had spent the day caring for my brother. The day before my brother was admitted into the hospital, I watched her as she enjoyed him. She was cooking, washing, or ironing on this Saturday. She was always doing one thing or another and did it very well. This day though, she took the time to sit down and talk and play with him hanging around her skirt tail.

My mom had scheduled the date for him to be admitted. That day came. She picked him up from my grandparents' house. She took him to the hospital, and they admitted him. They had scheduled to operate on him early the next morning. They never got the chance. They prepped and medicated him that morning. He went to the operation room. He never woke up. He died.

I was at my grandparents' house. This was the morning after they admitted him. The phone began to ring. I said to my grandparents "My baby brother had died" before the phone was answered. The voice on the other end of the telephone corroborated what I had said. I knew, somehow, I knew.

My grandma took a whole year to stop grieving over my baby brother Darren. He was one of her heartstrings and very special.

I had to accompany my mom to the hospital to view his body. I missed him already. I went home to my mom's house. I just walked around. I couldn't talk.

I left the house and went to the playground. I recalled telling a friend who persisted to ask me what was wrong. I told her that my brother had died and walked away from her.

In the coming days, I was distraught. There was the wake with many of our family and neighbors. Then there was the sad funeral. There were so many salutations from people that didn't even know him. Then there was a picture of him in the casket that someone took and gave to my mother. It was this picture that my mom cried over often.

All this resulted in a great big loss for me. I was not responsible, but why him?

I cried all night. I then remembered his smile. I cried no more.

CHAPTER 23

I got through with my school year. I passed. Now I will be going into the eighth grade. I no longer have to take all my cousins to the movies on Sundays. I get to do pretty much as I please.

I worked on tobacco again that summer. I still spent some weekends with my grandparents.

On Sundays after church, I was permitted to go to the skating palace. I learned to skate on the streets already, so skating was fun. I didn't fall too much. Summer is now over so I no longer worked on tobacco. My school year starts and I go to work for one of my uncles after school now. I now worked for another one of my uncles, Usher. I worked in his antique shop. He had all kinds of old things. He had clocks, watches, dishes, furniture, etc. We don't seem to sell much but he is open every day. I dust, swept, and put prices on things for him. He pays me. So I am happy.

I had family in Stowe Village. I had two aunts and several cousins living there. I get to visit my aunts and cousins in Stowe Village often as well. So I get to hang out with my cousins that live there. I have several major fights in Bellevue Square and Stowe Village.

These aunts, my mom, and my uncles had weekend parties. My cousins and I all spent the night then. There was always a bunch of us in one bedroom. We would peek out the door and watch them party. They sold liquor and food. Us kids all spent the night together, of course. The grown-ups would check on us frequently. We slept where we could fit in. We had plenty of blankets and pillows. So I had to visit my family in Stowe Village whether I wanted to or not.

I soon stopped going out of doors in Stowe Village alone. Several of the girls who lived there thought I wanted their boyfriends so they would approach me with that nonsense. When my word was never good enough, they blamed me because I was liked by their friends. It usually ended up with me having to fight one of them. However, my older male cousins had friends there that knew me. Therefore, someone always seemed to be around that had my back. They always saw to it that it was a fair fight. I had skills and I had to use them. Lillie was not the one you told you had a fight and didn't win. If you told her that, then you got beat again.

I pretty much had to establish my territorial rights. I could now walk through there or wherever without being bothered. I was liked, but there was always someone who wanted to try me. There was always someone that I had to prove myself to.

I had pretty nice clothing, and my aunt was a hairdresser, so I was always clean and my hair was okay, even though I still had not developed much.

I had facial scars: a cut under my nose, straight across, over my lip; I had a cut from the bridge of my nose straight up to over my eye; and I had a cut from under my eye down to my cheekbone. The color had come back. My eyebrows have finally grown back. I didn't look so bad now after all that.

CHAPTER 24

She is now really back to heaven or hell. She realized that Bellevue Square was full of drugs, gang harassment, and peer pressures.

She now had two sets of friends. She has the slow ones and the fast one.

Mariea joined the glee club. She was in the marching patrol for two years with the smaller kid's groups. She still had to really think about her actions. She now spent most of her weekdays at her grandparents, since it was closer to her school.

Her friends were starting to go out on weekends. Her chances of doing that were best at her mom's house. Therefore, she spent most of her weekends there.

She drifted from the big girls who smoked, drank a little, and by now had boyfriends. To the little girls, less mature. The little girls had curfews like she did. They were still just playing with the boys. They were not doing anything more serious than that.

Then there were the big girls, her older friends. These friends were the ones who drank. They smoked and ran around with older men. She was accepted by all the groups because she sometimes tried to do some of the things they all did

She drifted between the two groups of friends. The older girls were friends of her male cousins. When she found herself in their presence, she was attentive. For she thought they knew quite a bit about drugs, sex, and boosting. They knew things that seemed exciting to her. She felt grown-up with them.

So she went downtown with one of them. They were shoplifting. She thought she could do it as well. She got caught boosting the first time. Her mother came to the police station and got her and took her to her grandparents' house. Her granddad whipped her with his suspenders, and that hurt her to her heart. There were no body aches. There was just pain in her heart. She had let him down. He told her if she needs something, anything, she could ask him for it. Just ask and don't steal.

She sometimes ran with her school friends. They seemed to be faster than she was. For instance at parties, they all seemed to have boyfriends. She didn't have a boyfriend. Therefore, she just mingled and partied. She had many male friends, but not in the same capacity as them.

So she went from the group her age they still played with games and boys to the older ones who were not playing anymore. She took it all as a fun expedition. A train of thought she would not think of using in the other group settings. They were serious. Now that's the streets for her. This was basically how she rolled when she was at her mother's house.

CHAPTER 25

When at her grandparents, she went to church most nights. The friends there seemed to be good and have good morals. They were good, even when they were out and seen partying. They were her good brothers and sisters, ones she could turn her back on and not worry. So the good is not really counted or even considered. Then you realize later. You even learn that they look upon you in the same light as you see them. It is that your soul is not cleansed. Neither are theirs.

This realization only comes when wrong is done by one of them outside the church in a natural setting. Then you start to think that we all are human.

I am beginning to feel like things are pretty good in my life right now. My grandparents are good to me. My mom and stepfather are doing pretty well. They are both working now.

My mom was born with a fibrous dysplasia which is a bone marrow disease. Therefore, she had several operations on her arms to fix her bones. She even had the back part of her femur bone partially removed from her leg. This was put into one of her arms. Therefore, she had difficulty keeping a job for too long.

In spite of all the difficulties, things seemed to be looking up at home. My sister and brother has been missing me. Yet we do talk on the phone often. I am not there much. My coaching seems to be paying off though. My little brother is looking out for my little sister. She would not fight back when someone bothered her. So without me there, my brother has her back.

I am home a few times a week. I do most of the grocery shopping. I do most of the laundry. When we had a washing machine, I hung the clothing on the clothesline. When we had no washing machine, I took our clothing to the Laundromat, but whichever they were able to watch or participate. We were all pleased with the interactions. It meant a lot for me to be there for all of us. It was fine with me. They respected me. We loved each other, and we understood each other. We acquired a mutual bond that was unbreakable.

CHAPTER 26

My mother allowed me to go to Keney Park to ice-skate often when I am at home. On the way home from skating, I always stopped at my relative's houses.

On this occasion, I go to my uncle Wil's house on Capon Street which is not too far from the park. They always cooked so they fed me really good food. This was the uncle who liked to have a garden in the summer. So he always had fresh vegetables that he raised at his home. This is the uncle who later got his hand caught in one of his lawn mower. It cut his fingers off. He was hospitalized. He died shortly afterward.

I would also stop by my aunt Mae's house on Nelson Street when I was going to my grandparents. She also fed me when I stopped by. She also taught me to cook sausage and potatoes in the oven with green peppers and onions. She has two daughters. I really loved being with them. We had much fun playing outside together. This is the aunt I got my organization skills from. Once when I was spending the night, she asked me to go get something out of the dresser drawer. That is when I realized that everything was organized in her house. There were socks here, panties there, shirts, dresses, and pants all had their place. Everything was in order. I was amazed.

However, I decided to take this procedure along with me for life. It never took long to find what I was looking for after that. I had order in all my belongings. I always knew now where it all was. It was all in its own place. It never took me long to find anything anymore. I adopted this process. I now had a sense of order with my time and my talents.

I would also stop by my aunt Skirt's house when I'm in the vicinity. She was now a pastor in her church. It is said that she was wild back in the day. I remember her for some of the things she used to tell me personally.

She used to say, "If you only have one pair of undergarments, you should wash them every night. So always keep a bar of Ivory soap."

CHAPTER 27

Winter is almost over and spring is starting to show its face. Today is Friday. Good Friday 1963.

I'm thirteen years old. I went to church to rehearse for my Easter speech along with my sister and brother. Afterward, I got my sister and brother a ride with one of our uncles' home.

I stopped by grandma's house. She was different today. She scolded me, real hard, because I had sent my siblings home. She very rarely had to scold me, so I was bewildered. I sat and pondered in the kitchen. She called me into the living room. She had finally calmed down.

She said to me, "You are growing up now. Don't you let those little boys make a fool of you."

I said, "Oh, Gram," and we embraced. I knew she wasn't angry anymore, so outside I want to play.

I found out shortly after that she needed her medicine. She had asthma. My uncle had not yet brought it to her. He finally delivered it in the early evening.

My aunt Mae had arrived with her two daughters. She lived just up the hill. I was allowed to spend the night at their house so she could do my hair. We stayed, and I played with her daughters until it was almost nightfall. It was now time to go to her house before it got dark. We said our goodbyes and headed up the hill to her house.

CHAPTER 28

We were not at her house very long, not even an hour. The phone rang. We had to go back to my grandparents' house. I didn't know why at that time. It wasn't until we got into the house that I found out.

My grandma had a heart attack. My uncle James still lived in the house with her. He was the first to discover that something was wrong with her. He gave her artificial respiration to no avail. He was heartbroken, totally distraught.

My grandmother died on Good Friday 1963. The ambulance took an hour to get there.

By the time the ambulance arrived, my aunts and uncles, even my mother, had started to arrive. They all had gone upstairs where she was. She was still laying in her bed.

I sat on the stairs in the hallway and cried. As they went up and came back down the stairs, everyone was crying. Someone made me get off the stairs and come into the kitchen. I inched around the corner. The kitchen was next to the stairwell. I sat underneath the telephone which was just around the corner from the stairs. The telephone would not stop ringing. It only stopped when someone was on it informing others of our tragedy. I could not go upstairs to the bathroom. I was terrified. My mom reassured me that my grandma had never hurt me in life and could do nothing now to hurt me.

I was sinking fast. While we all waited for the hospital to call and say it was so. Her death was a loss for me. I had drawn so much strength from this lady.

Now, I would have no one who could tell me little things that meant so much more. She made me think. I could never figure out how she became so wise, with such a little amount of formal education. Life had taught her. She was married at thirteen years old. She had raised thirteen children. She knew what life was all about for her. So it was easy for her to teach me things.

Who would help me now when I needed to be heard? My grandma always understood. I wanted to go upstairs to the bathroom to get away from my people.

I was afraid of going upstairs and not feel her presence. Not hear her voice. But I did go upstairs. I did feel her presence. I could still hear her words. I still knew of her perseverance. So I will persevere. I will go through hell. I will just be dancing to a different drummer. Without her to soften my life, it was going to be even harder for me though.

I didn't want any of the material things they were all now claiming. I didn't need anything material to remind me of the thirteen years with that precious jewel. I watched them start to claim her belongings even before she was legally declared dead. My aunts were busy.

So I sat in the kitchen. The ambulance finally came and took grandma away. I silently wept. I sat unnoticed.

Then my uncle Frank from New York arrived. He walked in. He looked at us and he knew. He went upstairs, ran back down screaming, "Ma-Ma!"

Someone told him what had happened and he ran out of the house. He beat on his car and wept in the street. He came in shortly but didn't calm down for hours.

My uncle Bud arrived from Georgia. He was different. He wore white shoes. There was something about him that was the same though. He looked like my other uncles. He had my grandpa's sense of humor, even more so. He told us of the South, how it was, and about our people there with him. I liked him a lot, even though he talked funny.

I saw the dawning of a new day. I was made to go get some rest.

CHAPTER 29

My rest did not come easy. I had only memories now to see me through. Those memories took me to dreamland. I awoke to find the house was still full of my family members. We ate breakfast, and I sat out on the stoop for I knew not what was in store for me now.

My grandparents' house had been a heaven for me. I now knew the real jungle of my mom's house in Bellevue Square was upon me. I would not have anywhere to retreat to. Then for me in the coming days, before and shortly thereafter, I wandered through the house aimlessly.

My grandmother's funeral was being planned now. I didn't want to hear them talk about it.

The day came. I rode in a car, but I saw nothing. We arrived at the church. I was seated. It was all a blur. Then we were at the site of the grave.

I thought of the sight of seeing my uncle Tom who was allowed to come accompanied by the security of the jail he was incarcerated in. He cried so hard at seeing his mother for the last time. He was not allowed to go to the burial site. I thought of the uncles from out of state who had not seen her for a long time. Now, they were seeing her for the last time.

I felt for one uncle the most. That was Uncle Jim who was still living with her at home. This is the uncle who taught me that Wednesday was spaghetti day and how to prepare it. He ended up in Norwich State Hospital due to his loss of his mother. He was never the same after that.

I did not dare think of me since I could see all the people who were closest to her falling apart. I knew I couldn't, for she had told me so much that could keep me together.

I wondered why they could not accept such goodness and could not manifest and continue to grow when the yoke was so very heavy and the burden never light in this life we live. I knew, I guess like all the rest, but I accepted that I had to stand, even when I fell. I had to stand. So I prayed for strength as I looked upon all of them.

CHAPTER 30

I finally stopped visiting my granddad every morning and afternoon. I started going straight home after school. I stopped seeing a few of my friends. I only saw them in school and on weekends. I spent time in the playroom doing various activities. I started visiting my friends at their homes. Boys started to be the thing to do. I played ring-a-levio, jump rope, and hopscotch during the day. Sometimes when I play, I declare war if there were enough participants to play with me. I went on trips with the marching patrol.

This was all fine but different from the church every night and prayer at my grandparents' house. I was now not living in a preacher's house. There was vice in my house. There were cousins having girls in the house who were not supposed to be there. There were the gamblers and drunks who were uninvited but welcomed. All this quickly made me more alert of the perils of life and my surroundings.

CHAPTER 31

I haven't talked much about my dancing, but I am still doing it. I now go to another dance school, the Artist Collective. This school was founded by Jackie McLean. I have now traded my acrobatics for African dance. I am still tapping though.

My friends are now slow, fast, and faster. They are all into different things. The slow group was now fading fast. So I have started to be with the fast and faster groups more often. The fast group is now really drinking and partying. I could take it or leave it. Sex for me at that point was not happening, even though I was wanted and pursued. I was steadfast, but the attention was great. I looked fair to meddling now, and my clothing was always okay.

I had gotten to be a regular with the fast group. However, the faster group had a few good or best friends of mine in it. This was until I got used to sitting in their houses. I was learning how to smoke cigarettes. I was sometimes sipping wine. I was told to stay away from the fast group, yet I would not obey. I thought that no one would ever find out.

I have had several jobs now. I presently work at the Institute of Living. I am fixing meals for the people who live in the institute. I took the bus to work. It stops right in front of my job.

My mom said, "At fourteen, a sixteen-year-old is too old for me to be hanging out with." My mom said for me to stay out of her house. She said, "You are going out to play. You should play outside or come up into your own house to play. Or you can just stay in the house."

I thought, *But she is my friend*. So that year, I was not listening, but I should have been. I visited my friend at her house anyways.

CHAPTER 32

One day, her brother-in-law and his friend were there when I arrived. My friend was preparing food. She prepared some tuna and macaroni salad.

We listened to loud music while they were drinking. I didn't drink anything. They did most of the loud talking. Some of the talk was fresh. I was enjoying myself though. The talk was different in mixed company. It was nothing like when it was just us girls. Time passed by. I needed to go to the bathroom. When things get tough, I usually go to the bathroom. The conversation was now on that level.

I excused myself and went to the bathroom. The bathroom was off the living room where we had been and down the hallway. I used the bathroom. However, when I opened the door to come out, my passage was blocked by the brother-in-law.

I tried to get past him. He wasn't budging. When he did move, it was just a little. It was just on the other side of a bedroom entrance.

"No, I don't want to come into the bedroom. No, don't touch me."

He proceeded to pick me up and throw me onto the bed. He climbed on top of me.

"Would you please stop! Stop!" I can't scream with the bedspread in my mouth. I fought, I hurt, and I cried, "Lord, Lord please, help me. I need you now."

I was finally allowed to leave the room when he had finished with me. I told my friend, and she told her sister who was his wife. They both said, for me to tell my mother. Day after day, I wanted to tell my mom, but it was never the right time. So time goes by.

I was walking by the pool hall on my way home shortly after this occurrence. There were men standing outside talking to each other.

One of the men said to the others, "She has some good stuff."

Then another one of the men said, "She is a child. So how do you know that about her?"

He said, "Because I had some of that."

The man asking the questions was one of my uncles, Tom. He was now out of jail. He was living with us in my mom's house.

He beat this man up badly. He then came home to my mom's house. He then sent one of my siblings to get me from outside.

CHAPTER 33

My uncle Tom asked me if something had happened to me. He asked if someone had touched me inappropriately. He asked when and where this occurred. I confessed gladly. I confessed even though the only thing I was guilty of was disobeying my mom. I told him everything. I was relieved finally to be able to get it out of me.

The police were called. They took my mom and I to the police station. They examined me at the police station. I felt raped again.

That was just the beginning. Those people from some agency kept coming. They kept coming day after day. They kept taking me away from home. My mom finally stopped going with me. I went with them alone. I get more examinations. I told them what happened to me over and over again. I told them the truth. I never changed my story because I could remember every detail. I told it over and over again just like it happened. I can never forget. I will never forget. Never!

The story got written up in the newspapers. There was no name given, just "a fourteen-year-old." He was arrested. They charged him with rape of a minor.

So once the story got out. People just knew somehow that it was me. They embarrassed me in the community. They talked about me in the grocery store like I wasn't even there. They pointed fingers at me when I passed by. Some of the grown-ups whispered as I walked by. I was ridiculed by many. Some of the other parents said that I could not play with their children.

I held my head up high because I soon accepted myself for who I knew I was. Some of these people even thought I was guilty though. They had the nerve to say so to my face. I maintained through it all with a whatever attitude. I was not guilty of anything except defying my mom. No one knew how I felt about all this but me. No one knew what hell I lived in every day.

CHAPTER 34

The day finally came for us to go to court about this case. The courtroom was full when we arrived. My grandpa went with my mom and I to court.

He said to me, "Just tell the truth."

I did again and again when they called me to do so.

Our court case was called. I was called to the stand to testify. I was sworn in on the Bible. They tried to make me feel guilty so many times. I told the truth. I told nothing but the truth. They finally allowed me to step down. I went back to my seat. My mom hugged me. I was trembling.

My girlfriend was called to the stand as a witness. This was my girlfriend whose house it happened in. She did not initially tell the story like it had happened. She did not tell the truth. She told lies for her family. The prosecutor pounded her. He said that this was not the story she had given them previously. I felt betrayed. They threatened her with a perjury charge. She finally admitted the true version of the incident. She told one version close to the one she had originally told them.

They finished questioning us. The plaintiff did not testify. They gave him eighteen months in jail. He did the time. They turned him loose.

This man, sometime after he was released from jail, came to my mom's house to visit. I answered the door. I was shocked to see him standing there. He wanted to come in to see my uncle. I stopped him at the door. He had the nerve to say he served his time for his crime. I slammed the door in his face.

CHAPTER 35

I was trying to go on with my life. Somehow, I had to continue to grow up, despite all obstacles. I was trying. While hanging out one afternoon, I had spotted a fellow that I might be interested in. He seemed to be around my age. He was singing in a hallway with a few other guys. He sang beautifully. I later found out that most of his family played instruments. I was intrigued with him. He was not interested in me then. That was okay. It was not important since he seemed to be a little slow anyways. He didn't seem to fit my fast mode, yet I thought, at first, that may have been the reason I might have chosen him.

Life was moving on. I had only missed a few beats of life. I had graduated from junior high school now. I had been kissed at a party by a fast young man. My slow friends were not ready. I don't know if I was either.

I kept finding myself in this singing young man's presence. He soon relinquished his attentions. I was shortly permitted to accompany him to some of his rehearsals and concerts. He sang with the vocal group, the Discounts. They were some local project young men who started singing on corners and in hallways. They sounded pretty good.

I started to find him to be in the sort of fast lane, yet he was somewhat slower than I was mentally. He was attractive, charming, and he knew it. Therefore, he had no problem getting young ladies. I had the problem. I figured he was my boyfriend and enough said. However, this factor later played a key role in our relationship.

The group he sang with were already friends of mine from school and marching patrol. Some of them were even very close male friends. So during his rehearsals, we would usually play around with each other. This behavior disturbed my beau. He was the jealous type, yet he flirted with most girls. Early in the relationship, I found out what was permissible for me. I did not abide by his wishes at all times. I had enough parents. I also love attention. So there were many instances where I was in his presence and he was far from being attentive. His attentions seemed more so than not to be somewhere else.

We started to have arguments often. Our arguments turned into fights. He liked to put his hands on me. He liked to hit me. He did not like his hits returned though. I did not like to be beat on by anyone. So I always fought back.

We broke up. We went back together. Nothing ever really changed. He had dropped out of school. He did not even work. He hung around street corners. He drank wine and he sang. He made some money singing in the streets and hallways. It was just enough to keep him in nice clothes and his hair processed.

Around this time, the Discounts stopped singing in the street and hallways. They were now singing pretty regularly in clubs like the Lenox Theater and Passion 500. This was a club for teenagers. So he was now making a little bit of money. He started to womanize more. He was a street-corner singer, a wine-drinking, fine, young man that I called mine. I still hung in there with him. I got him, but so did a number of others. I got him all right.

I came out of high school with two of his children.

The End
(To Be Continued)

Volume 2

FOREWORD

Mariea was finding out that her heritage gave her the strength to persevere.

She was with the strength and endurance of her African blood. She had the wits and ingenuity of her Indian descent. She was witty and strong.

Her mother and her siblings taught her so many different ways of coping with the daily endeavors in life. She was headstrong. She was a pioneer of sorts. She was forever exploring new avenues and feared very little. She went places she did not know about. She did things she should not have. She chalked a lot of things up to experience. Life was teaching her in a way she could have never imagined.

She took life in strides, yet most times, she came out ahead of the game. She refused to let life take her. She was determined to take life and gain from the takings.

She persevered on a path. She was aiming for something better than what stared her in the face.

INTRODUCTION

She is still pushing while thriving for excellence by being and doing the best she knows how.

Mariea was moving on in this life. She never imagined it would be turning out the way it was.

She had experienced the deaths of several loved ones. She had established herself in several of her different worlds. She was moving forward in spite of all the obstacles that found themselves in her way.

She had no idea where she was going. She just knew she had to keep on going.

Her destiny was already planned before she realized she had to live it to the fullest.

So now she is in hell more than she is in heaven as she pursues the inevitable.

S. Aminiah Nialiah, also known as Saundra Foster

CHAPTER 1

Mariea was now in high school. She attended Hartford Public High School.

She no longer worked on tobacco in the summers. Her uncle's antique shop has now gone out of business. She now has a part-time job at the Institute of Living. She fed the clients there. These clients were people that could not live at home or on their own for one reason or another.

She has gotten good at her dancing at the Artist Collectives. She was doing regular performances in various venues. Most of which are tap dances. She had no problem learning routines or remembering them. She, in spite of all the obstacles in her life, still found joy and peace in her dance.

She had regular marching patrol meetings at the Elks club on Canton Street. She practiced with the marching patrol in Arsenal School's yard during the week and on weekends. They march in many city parades. She traveled with the marching patrol and marching band to those parades in various places. They party on the bus when returning after the parades.

They had marched in a parade in Meriden. This afforded them to get an invitation to march in a parade in Waterbury in the near future.

This Elks Club where they had their meetings was next door to Mary Brooks's family's Muslim restaurant. This was where she got beef patties on occasions. That was next door to Nicks Cleaners which was next to Nellies' grocery store. This store had everything from fresh meats to canned goods and fruit. This was the store where they had whispered about her when she had gotten raped.

As we move on up the block, there was the barbershop that did the slick processes for the males. The record shop owned by Roz next to that and a shoe store. As we proceed around the corner, there was

Nicks' package store, a supermarket, and then the poolroom. The people who hung outside the poolroom no longer whisper when she walked by. They now knew that she had relatives that hung in there.

CHAPTER 2

Now, I should say that her relatives were still in and out of her mother's house. Some of her relatives were into drugs and alcohol. The others were just plain thieves.

Her Aunt Lu visited regularly. She was different. She talked trash to everyone. She drank and told funny stories. She also kept birds at her apartment. She had a pigeon once when I went over. The next time I went over there, she didn't have it. My mom said she cooked it and ate it. I never knew if that was true, but the pigeon was gone.

The time for her to march in Waterbury had come. She had brought her marching patrol uniform to the cleaners. She went and got it out of the cleaners. She brought it home and she hung it up in her kitchen on the clothesline. This was in preparation for her departure for the parade. When the time came for her to depart, the uniform had disappeared. One of her family members had taken it. No one noticed that it was gone. No one saw who took it. She was permitted to go on the trip, but she could not march.

Mariea knew who took her uniform. He was the same cousin that would molest her and make her do all kinds of other things. He would do this whenever she was at her grandparents' house. She hated to be left alone in their house with him there. He would also steal meat out of her mother's freezer.

She was no longer that little girl. She had been taken advantage of by others now. She had no fear of him anymore. She was so tired of being taken advantage of. She was tired of suffering because of other people's actions toward her.

She had worked hard and saved to pay for her uniform. Now she would have to get another one made and pay again for it.

She was at home the next time he came meandering into her mother's apartment to visit. She confronted him about the uniform. He said he didn't take it. He said he wouldn't do such a thing to her. She picked up a knife. She threatened him with the knife and called him a liar. She told him to leave her mother's house and not to return without returning her property. He pleaded with her not to cut him and he left.

The uniform reappeared on the line in the kitchen after a couple of days from that.

He was nowhere to be found.

CHAPTER 3

Mariea still got into many fights. She would never back down from a challenge. People always had something to beef about with her. She had street fights. She had school fights. She even fought a family of four who were trying to bully her siblings.

Her brother was getting big now. Yet she still fought for him. Until one day, the Magnificent Twenties gang were after him. He came home and told her. She had a consultation with him. She let him know that she had taught him to fight back. She reiterated that she was a girl and fighting all these boys was not fair to her or proper. Even though, she won most of the fights she had with boys. It was time for him to step up.

The group of males came to confront him. He was well-advised as to what they were going to do. She and her brother stood back-to-back and fought with all they had. They both got hurt, but they kept on fighting. They hurt a few of them as well. The crowd soon backed off them. This must have been some kind of initiation. He was soon allowed to be in the Magnificent Twenties after that.

I now go to Parker Center for recreation. I stop by to check on my granddad often in Nelton Court. He was not doing so well without my grandma. He finally moved to the Bellevue Square project where I live. He stayed there for quite some time. I could visit him daily since he was just down the hill from me. That was before he fell and broke his hip bone and had to go live in one of my aunts' houses. This aunt was my mother's sister who used to look under my dress every time I came to see my grandad. She was a minister in the church I now attended.

She wanted to make sure I remembered to have on clean panties.

CHAPTER 4

I still attend church on occasion with my grandfather. I attend Christ Church of Deliverance on Acton Street. This was the church where one of my aunts and an uncle were preachers, until my granddad opened his own church, Zion Apostolic Church of Christ.

I truly let God into my life at thirteen. I knew there had to be a power greater than me. That power that kept me rising instead of sinking in some of my despair. It had to be God's power. That was around the time I came to the realization that sometimes in my life, lemons made into lemonade still did not taste good. Not even when I tried my best to sweeten them.

I prayed. I prayed for my family. I prayed for my surroundings. I prayed when I am out alone at night. I prayed when I am at home at night. I prayed mostly for my well-being and that tomorrow will be a better day for me.

I experienced some gang pressures. I refused to join any of the gangs that approached me. I have worked tobacco for several summers now. So I can now put some of my money into the bank.

I didn't realize it, but I grew this summer. Upon arriving to my gym class when school started, they did their yearly measurements on all the students. I had grown from four feet, eleven inches to five feet, seven inches. To my own amazement, I was tall and not so short anymore. I now knew why I didn't have to ask anyone to get things off the top shelf for me anymore. My shoe size had changed, but I still hadn't noticed my height changing. I must not have gained much weight because my clothes still fit.

Then it really started to occur to me. When I went to marching patrol, they moved me from one spot to another since the lines were arranged by height. The lines of males and females were all arranged by your height. I now had to learn the routine from another perspective. That was no problem. It was all dancing through marching steps anyways.

CHAPTER 5

My dad now lives in New York. He had to move from Charter Oak Terrace in Hartford. He was an air records control person with the airlines. His job was transferred to New York, so he had to move there.

Here we go again. I seem to always be on the move. So if I was not visiting my family members in Connecticut, I was home in Bellevue Square. I would sit in the schoolyard some evening after work. It was summer no classes, work, save money. I was wilding. It was a moderate wild, because everything I do is in moderation. So in my orderly form of moderation I go so far then I turn around. That is because I will never see where the end is if I don't stay alive.

I was permitted to take Greyhound Bus trips to New York to see my dad and my other siblings. I can now take the subway from the bus station and walk to their house. Sometimes, my brothers would meet me. We hang out in the streets of New York. We also party, get high off weed, and drink beer.

My dad now owned several houses. I get to go with him when he would go to pick up his rent from his tenants. The government decided to cut back on air records controllers. So he was one of the last people in and one of the first out. He lost that job because of government cuts. He had to find new employment. He found a job working for the state of New York. He now worked for the New York transit system on the subways.

My dad sometimes took me to the Apollo on Wednesday nights in the summer. We would ride the subway to the city of Manhattan from Long Island. We would eat dinner in the city. We would then stop and get overripe tomatoes. Then we would proceed to the Apollo Theater for amateur night. That was during the time when you could still throw tomatoes at the people onstage who were not doing good.

My dad would cook for us at other times. He taught me how to make his infamous chili. He planted fruit trees, apple, peach, and pear, in an effort to keep me out of other people's trees. He also had a grapevine and a huge fresh vegetable garden. I would always leave New York to go home to Connecticut with a bag of fresh fruit.

I liked to go across the street from his house to the park and play handball. I was very good at it, but we didn't play it in Connecticut. In Connecticut I would use a tennis court wall until someone wanted to play tennis on it.

I enjoyed being in New York. I didn't have to fight so much. My siblings were fun to be around. There were so many of us and most of the people we were around were their friends. We gambled some, drank some, and soon it was time for me to return to Hartford.

Most of the time when I returned home, my dad would drive me back in his car with my siblings. They would visit with my other parents before returning to New York.

CHAPTER 6

I was now back to the reality of my current life in Bellevue Square.

I had a few friends who always gave football game parties so I would attend those. We would eat, drink, and enjoy each other. There would usually be a houseful of both males and females.

I also was allowed to go to Keney Park to ice-skate. I usually walked home by way of my family's houses and eat. I can skate very well. I even had enough money saved to purchase a secondhand pair of my own ice skates.

I was permitted to go to Parker Memorial Recreation center some evenings. This was located near Stowe Village. I found out something from a friend of mine just before the center was about to close. I found out that there were some girls from Stowe Village who were waiting for me to come outside. They were overheard discussing this.

I left out of the center and proceeded to go up the hill. I acted like I didn't know anything. That is when the crowd started to gather behind me. They called me out by name. I stopped walking. I turn around and they approach me with some nonsense. One of them takes the lead as she gets in my face. It ended up with me having to fight them off. They tried to put their best girls on me. Yes, it became two against one. I was winning though. I fought with everything that I had. That was when male friends of my cousins appeared. There were two guys who also lived in Stowe Village and knew us all. They broke the fight up. These two fellows escorted me part of the way home. They inquired as to whether I was okay. I was.

When I arrived home, I told my mom about the fight. My mom asked me if I won, I told her yes. I avoided having to get whipped from her.

I never get tired of fighting. I had skills learned from my male cousins. I had to defend myself at all times. Shoot your best shot.

Not too long after that, I was going home from the recreation center. I was just around the corner from my building when I am approached by this girl I had never seen before. She asked me if Herb was my boyfriend. I said yes.

She proceeded to punch me in the face. She then said I had better leave him alone. She said that he did not belong to me. She said all this after punching me in the face. I jumped on her with both hands and feet. We fought hard. I thought that I was winning though. I was on top.

My friends stopped the fight because the police had arrived. My friends took me into the building right next to us. They lived in this building. They were taking me up to the top floor to their apartment. Before we could get to the top floor, I realized that this girl was coming up the stairs behind us. She was in front of her friends. I turned around and kicked her back down the stairs. I proceeded to go down and ram her head through the hallway window.

I never saw the police coming. That is when the police approached me with the handcuffs. They handcuffed me. That is when they realized that I was bleeding. My pant leg was sopping wet with blood. When I was on top of her beating her she was cutting my leg and I never felt it.

I was taken to the hospital before being taken to jail. I found out that I had been cut in two places on my left leg. The two cuts were just above my knee on the inside of my thigh just above my knee. I received fifty-six stitches and a case for assault and battery. The case was later dropped.

However, I was arrested for defending myself.

My leg took a while to heal. After the stitches were removed, it hurt to bend it when I walked, but I persevered with the pain.

CHAPTER 7

I get up early every morning to go to school. I walked to Hartford High school after picking up one of my girlfriends named Bev. I always had to wait for her until her mother finished sewing her outfit to wear that day. Her mother was sewing with that same sewing machine that she would later give to me. That was when she bought a new one. This was because it was in good condition and her daughter had no interest in sewing. She asked me if I wanted it one day. Thanks be to God.

Bev and I go way back to the days when we went to Camp Courant every morning in the summers. We ate our lunches together there of the choke sandwiches which are peanut butter and jelly. We swam together, we did arts and crafts, and we would swing on the maypole together. I always waited in line for my turn to do the maypole. We made a lot of pot holders and an apron in their arts-and-craft classes.

There were many girls there from Charter Oak projects. They remembered me from the days spent there at my dad's house. We never got along, but we didn't fight. We argued a lot though. They would do things like try to get ahead of me in lines. They talked junk so I would hear them, but I would ignore them. I didn't want to get kicked out of camp to spend my days in the project doing nothing.

My school days were complicated. I sewed, cooked, and I also had the regular high school classes with very few friends. There are many people in Hartford High School who remembered me from other places. Some are the girls from Charter Oak. They remember way back when we met at Camp Courant. They still held grudges. I had to fight one of them again. My mother was not pleased with me. I got kicked out of school. I got suspended for two weeks.

She analyzed the situation. I was allowed to transfer now to Weaver High School before the two weeks were over.

CHAPTER 8

I completed the school year at Weaver High School.

I worked my way through the summer. I went back to Weaver High School at the beginning of the school year. I got up early. I would walk to school alone most days. I kept a low profile. I did my schoolwork and I would leave.

Fall came and then winter. I then went to work for the post office for their Christmas season. This was a very different experience. There was mail everywhere. I got to see how they move the mail on a daily basis and throughout the night. They would sort mail by hand and by machines. There are machines for local mail and out of state mail. They had bagging areas where the mail is thrown into bags for world mail. They had shipping and loading docks. They had trucks coming and going all the time. They had various shifts to work. I would have to work wherever I was needed the most. You are always watched while working. You were watched for stealing or mishandling mail, which is a federal offense. The pay was good, but you worked very long hours.

I had stopped working for the Institute of Living by that time.

So at the beginning of the year, I went to work for Pratt and Whitney washing dishes and making salads. I was allowed to take the bus to work after school and back home at night since it was still early evening.

CHAPTER 9

I started to babysit for my next-door neighbors on the weekends. I only had to go out of my kitchen door 5 steps to their door.

One particular Saturday night, I arrived at their apartment around 7:00 p.m. The two children, a boy and a girl, had already eaten. I bathed them and put them to bed for the night. At about eight thirty or nine o'clock, once the children were asleep, I left their apartment. I was going to a house party. This party was not in the area. This party was kind of far away. I partied most of the evening. I left to go home and almost made it home.

About a block from my house, there stood my mother. She called to me. She told me I had better not run from her. She proceeded to whip me all the way home. She asked what was I thinking putting those kid's lives in jeopardy by leaving them alone. I didn't think about that. I thought I'm going to have me some fun, and I really thought I could get away with it. That was a very wrong choice.

I lost that job and a half of the pay for that night. I got the whipping and was put under punishment. I had a good time, but it was not worth what I paid for the fun.

CHAPTER 10

I am still walking to Weaver High School just like I had walked to Hartford High School. I walked in all types of weather. We went to school in all types of weather. The schools were open when the weather was bad. During winter storms, they were open. They seemed to only close when the weather was bad enough for a boiler burst. So when there was no heat in the school, you get to leave to go home then and only then.

Things were better. I spent my time doing what I needed to do for me. I worked and went to school. I hung out in the schoolyard with a bunch of friends and associates.

I was still seeing that same guy who I had chased behind. He started coming around more. My family accepted him. He even drank wine with my stepfather. He still didn't have a job, but I refused to give him any of my money. He seemed to always be somewhere around. I visited him at his house some times. He had a family of instrumentalist. Some played drums, some played horns. He sang. He was one of fifteen children. Most of his brothers and sisters were still living in the same house as he. They always had a lot of activities going on in his house.

He was also at my house most nights. He even spent some nights at my house. I really disliked this factor. He never asked my opinion on it though.

One night, we were watching TV with both my mom and step-father. A knock came on the kitchen door. It was a young man asking for him. I called him to the door. I heard the guy say something to the effect that, "Herb should leave his girlfriend alone."

I closed the door thinking, *Uh-huh, your stuff is catching up with you.*

Shortly afterward, Herb entered back into the house. He was bleeding from his neck. That man had cut his throat. My mom put a towel around his neck and called for an ambulance. He went to the hospital in the ambulance. He stayed a long time before he was released. I visited him in the hospital and when he was allowed to go home.

He recovered from that throat cutting, but I don't think it mended his ways. He was still womanizing. It didn't affect his singing voice. So he was still singing to charm the ladies.

CHAPTER 11

I stayed at Weaver for a year. I did not like it. I went back to Hartford High and they let me back in with stipulations for the upcoming year. No fighting, among other things.

I still worked at Pratt and Whitney, washing dishes and sometimes making salads.

I was now in the eleventh grade. I still worked for the post office for another Christmas season.

I became pregnant that winter, in January, after the holidays were all over. I never thought about or even knew I ever wanted children. Much less, I did not want a man to wait on. I especially did not want one who was not offering me very much. He only had himself to give and he thought that was a lot.

I was too blind to see the forest for the tree.

I was ashamed of doing stuff in my parents' house. We would say our good nights when he was leaving in the kitchen at the door. This was on the other side of the refrigerator which you had to walk around to see us at the door. No one ever came around it.

My mother was kind. My aunts were sympathetic. My friends called me a fool. I went to school every day and I worked odd jobs. I gained some weight. I started to get sick often. I was ashamed of myself at sixteen.

I was not ready to be a parent. This should not be happening to me. Actions have consequences. I was paying for my actions because I was going to have this baby.

I was aware of my body changing. I had to quit dancing. This tore my heart apart. I went to school, reluctantly sick. I threw up all day from morning to night. I still kept going to school. I went to work, and I prayed. I was miserable. I now had to stay home and rest when I wasn't working or going to school.

CHAPTER 12

When I awoke one particular day, I felt really bad. I ate a light breakfast, and I left home. I felt a little queasy while walking to school, but I kept on going. I went to school this particular day not feeling good at all. I went to my homeroom, then to my first period class. My breakfast came up in the classroom. I was so embarrassed.

I was ashamed of myself. My classmates were so attentive. My teacher called the janitor. My teacher then sent me to the nurses' office. The nurse talked to me. I told her about my condition. She then made a suggestion. She suggested that I leave Hartford High School.

So after our conversation, the nurse called and enrolled me in an alternative learning center for pregnant girls around my age. This association was connected to the Hartford public school system. I was grateful.

I was sent home for that day. I discussed this with my mother. She was pleased that I would be continuing my education.

This new school of sorts was on Upper Albany Avenue. This whole ordeal was tough on me physically and mentally.

In the midst of all this confusion I was having within myself, there was my beau still undaunted by the fact of fatherhood. He was still acting like a complete asinine person. We didn't do many things together. We didn't go many places together because he rarely had any money. He seemed not concerned at all with my physical condition. He also still thought he could hit me. Physically and mentally he abused me.

I was really in this all alone, with the exception of my mother. She was very concerned, but I didn't want her worrying about me.

I was literally a fool for love. I had no idea that I was being used while being abused.

CHAPTER 13

I was at this school for some time now. It wasn't so bad since every one of the students was in the same predicament. We were all expecting babies. The facility fed us lunch. We could eat and drink in class. We could even take naps. There were new students coming in all the time.

One day, a girl from the Bellevue Square project where I lived registered at this facility. She looked sort of familiar. I then knew she looked familiar because she lived a couple of houses from where I lived.

It didn't take too long to find out that we were more connected than just living in the same project. I found out that we were pregnant by the same person. The girls in the facility were very happy to tell me. They were waiting for a reaction. I didn't give them any satisfaction or reaction to the information. I was dead inside right then.

When I got home, I called him to ask him to come over. When he arrived, I questioned him about the situation. He denied it. That was a barefaced lie. It only proved that he was a liar, a cheater and was not worthy of my affection.

Yet I thought, *What could I do, but accept the fact since I already knew he was a womanizer?*

I did know, deep down inside that this was not an accident. I also knew that neither would it be an accident for my baby to have a sibling six months younger, but not from me.

I kept telling myself that God knew what he was doing. I didn't even know what I was doing. I was just going through the motions, trying to stay alive and healthy for the one I was carrying with the whole world watching.

CHAPTER 14

One day when I arrived at home, shortly after that incident, Herb was there. I didn't know why. He wanted to ask me if I would go out with him on Saturday night.

I said where. He said would you please never telling me where we would be going. I consented. In spite of not feeling well, I was curious.

Saturday came. He and I went to a house party together. It was a long way from where we lived. We walked because he didn't have a ride. I was fat now. I was about six months pregnant, plump, and just a little fat.

When we arrived at the house, I realized that I knew the people who lived there. They happened to be friends of mine from one of the schools I had gone to.

I was greeted by the host and many of the other people there.

Herb found me a seat on a couch in the living room. Most of the people were already partying. He proceeded to search out and pursued some young lady. He entertained this young lady out on the back porch all the time we were at this party.

Several of my friends were there. My friends were very attentive. They brought me food and drinks. They held conversations with me off and on. One of his female cousins felt very bad about my situation. She knew something was going on. She felt so bad that she told me what was going on. She also advised me to leave him alone.

When the party was coming to an end, he returned to the couch where I was. He said it's time to leave.

I said, "Oh yeah. I haven't had my dance yet."

He danced with me.

CHAPTER 15

We said our goodbyes and headed out of the door. Upon leaving the party, I confronted him with the accusations.

"First, you leave me sitting on the couch all night. Then you party all night with someone else."

He acted as though the incident never happened. I continued to question him about it. He then proceeded to knock me down in some bushes on the side of the street. It was kind of hard for me to get up. During this time, a few of my female friends assisted me in getting up off the ground. They asked if I was okay. I said yes in spite of myself.

I then noticed that a few of my male friends who were also leaving the party accosted him. They were all around him. I don't know what was said or done. At that time, I was approached by another male that I knew. He offered to take me home in his car. I accepted the ride. During the ride, he talked to me as a male and as a friend. He told me I didn't deserve to be treated that way. He also told me that I didn't have to accept such treatment from anyone.

I cried, and he held me.

Herb later arrived at my home, acting like none of this ever happened. He acted as though he was innocent all the way. I tolerated him that late evening for a short time. However, he had to go home or wherever he had to go. He just had to leave.

CHAPTER 16

Now I have never considered myself as being a glutton for punishment, yet the circumstances surrounding and underlying the events in this relationship would state otherwise. My current circumstance told me that is exactly what I am doing.

It made me feel like I am nothing, yet I keep telling myself that I believe he is a prized possession. No matter what anyone said, I cared. I kept caring and holding on. I prayed for him often, but God had this. So I continued in a relationship that was one-sided. He would say that he had feelings for me, but his actions spoke much louder than his words. We went through the motions. But in hindsight, I knew it was unhealthy. It was downright toxic, but I didn't have much to judge it by then.

I knew I loved myself. I knew my siblings loved me. I knew my family members loved me. I had no clue what his feelings for me were. I just knew that he kept coming around, and I kept letting him be around me.

CHAPTER 17

I had now completed the eleventh grade. My grades were not too bad. I passed.

I went to work for the tax department that summer. They paid more than Pratt and Whitney did, and I wasn't washing dishes. I was doing accounting work.

I walked to and from work that summer. I was sick most days, throwing up on the street. Some mornings, I would get up to the corner and have to hold on to a light pole to keep from passing out. I would be praying, waiting until it subsided. Then I would continue down the street not feeling dizzy anymore.

My boss was very considerate and understanding. I guess he looked at me and had compassion. Maybe he knew I needed this job to make it past where I now found myself. He allowed me to spend most of my afternoons in the bathroom. He never said anything when I slept at my table or barfed in the stairwell. He never once said anything about my condition at all. He just made sure I got paid.

I worked hard, in spite of the circumstances of my condition. I was always on time, and I always met my deadlines. My work was completed. He would congratulate me on that effort.

He was definitely a godsent person.

CHAPTER 18

I regularly attended my doctor appointments. I knew the time was getting close.

Summer came to an end and so did my job with the tax department.

I am now in the twelfth grade. I am back at Hartford High School's alternative setting. I could not attend regular school yet. My classes were kind of hard. I finished Algebra II last year. I am taking trigonometry and American history and they were both giving me a fit. I tried to work with a tutor; however, I am still struggling.

I was working hard to keep my head above water with so much madness. That may have been a good thing. I was not fighting with anyone at the present time. I even made some new friends.

The official Hartford High School was now under reconstruction. Therefore, we had split sessions at the alternative school just like the official school. I was fortunate enough to get the early session. So I had a part-time job in the afternoons working in an office. I seem to be able to find work and to keep money in my pocket and in the bank.

It was hot and humid during the month of October. This was only one month after returning to school. Summer had faded, but I was still overheated most of the time.

I still played cards. So my sister and I walked to her godfather's to play some cards with him. He fed us some pig feet and potatoes salad. We played cards most of the night. I was very uncomfortable. I kept on having to go to the bathroom. He finally sent us home in a cab and told me to get some rest. I had won us some money though.

I went to bed, but I still had to keep going to the bathroom. I had been at home for about two hours. I went to the bathroom again. This time I looked into the toilet, and there was blood. I called to my mom to come see. She said my water had broken. She called me an ambulance.

CHAPTER 19

The ambulance came. I was on my way to Hartford hospital. I went to Hartford hospital in the ambulance alone. My mom stayed to watch the children.

The ambulance ride was not bad. I realized that this part of my life was my own. I really was all alone. I had God with me and that was all I wanted and needed. I prayed for myself and my oncoming baby. I was still a kid, but growing to be a woman fast. I knew that this woman would have to care for this child that she was about to give birth to. I didn't know how I would do it, but I knew that I had no other choice.

I was bringing this child into the world. This is a cruel world that doesn't care about me. I knew at that moment, on that ambulance ride, that my whole life had changed. I would not be by myself. I could no longer be thinking only for myself or about myself. I would have to fed, clothe, and care for me, to be able to take care of a child.

I was examined upon arrival at the hospital. They said I was too far gone to have local anesthesia. I would have to get a spinal injection. That turned out to be okay. I was able to stay awake for the delivery. There were no complications with birth. They talked to me during the whole process. They wanted to know how I felt. I felt no pain. I felt like this part of my situation is almost over.

They wanted to know what I wanted to have.

I wanted to have a healthy baby.

CHAPTER 20

My baby girl was born. My daughter weighed five pounds fifteen ounces. She was so beautiful with a headful of curly hair. I named her Wonie. These were glorious moments, yet they were so full of uncertainties. I checked for fingers and toes. They were all there. She appeared to be perfect, yet the doctors said she had a heart defect.

My family visited me. My mom brought my siblings. They all commented on how beautiful my baby was. Her father came to visit as well, acting like he always does, foolish. With him, one thing lead to another and we argued. He was upsetting me in the hospital and I asked him to leave which he gladly did. I didn't think he wanted to be there anyways.

I was able to go home after three days. Herb visited me at home. He never asked if I needed anything for myself or the baby. He never brought anything either.

I had saved enough money to buy the crib and whatever else she needed. I asked no one for anything. I asked my mom for assistance. She helped me learn how to fix the formula. She helped me learn how to bathe my child. Things were going as well as could be expected.

I soon started my healing process, my mom continued to help when I needed it. She also took care of my baby while I handled my other business affairs.

CHAPTER 21

It was now November, around Thanksgiving. I have been out of school for too long. I went back to the big house of Hartford High School. I went back to school just before the holiday season started. I barely knew what was going on in my classes. I am so far behind in all my subjects. I felt so lost, but I was trying to keep up to make up for lost time. It doesn't seem to be working though. I scored very low on a test. I didn't give up on this losing battle, but I was sinking.

My mom now had her hands full with me back in school. I really didn't trust anyone else to take care of my baby.

Her father wanted to take her places with him. I didn't trust him, but I allowed him. He just wanted to show her off. Yet some of the people whom he let attend to her while she was out with him were less than desirable. I confronted him about this point along with so many other points. He could not accept my viewpoints. Nevertheless, I limited his taking her out to places without me. He could only hem and haw about it. I always had an excuse not to let him take her far or for too long.

Therefore, not much had changed in our relationship after I had the child. If anything, they were probably worst.

I loved her so dearly. She was so small, so pretty, fragile, and special.

CHAPTER 22

I felt as though my world was caving in on me shortly after the holidays were over. It was because before my baby turned three months old, I was with child again. No not again.

I was despondent. I did not wish this condition to exist again. I hated myself and him. I worked hard. I hoped it would go away. I knew girls who did something about this condition. However, I could not bring myself to that.

Fuel, at this point, got added to my personal fires. It is said that he doesn't give you more than you can handle. I personally was not trying to hear that right now. I was overwhelmed to say the least.

My baby girl became ill one evening. She had never been ill before. She had sensitive skin. So I always used medicated or Ivory soap. She had never caught a cold, so she appeared, to me, to be healthy and beautiful. She was so precious. She helped me through the hard times, for I was all she had. This thought gave me strength. Yet this evening in question, she threw up her dinner. That was strange, for she always ate well.

I thought, *Maybe she had eaten too much?*

So off to bed she went.

Now I was still working and going to school. I was in the twelfth grade. I was still struggling very much right about now to get my grades back up.

That night went by uninterrupted. My baby did not awaken the next morning. Before I got ready to leave, I advised my mother, "If her breakfast didn't stay down, to take her to the hospital."

Her breakfast didn't stay down. My mom took her to the hospital. I called home on my break. I found out that they had kept my baby in the hospital.

I went to the hospital when I got out of school. They explained to me the problem. She ended up staying in the hospital for seven days. The doctor said she had pneumonia.

CHAPTER 23

I visited her and held her in between school and work every day. She would cry when I had to leave. She was almost six months old.

The day finally came for me to take her home. The nurse informed me, after I had gotten her dressed, that I had to speak to the doctor before taking her home. I know people have to be released by the doctor before leaving the hospital, so I anticipated that they wanted to tell me about her diet going forward or something to that effect. I was ill-prepared for what he told me.

The doctor informed me that my baby was born with a hole in her heart. The hole had now gotten to be big enough to leak. This hole was now leaking blood through a vessel to her lungs. The lungs were filling up. This is what gave the pneumonia diagnosis. This was why she had gotten sick in the first place. Her lungs were congested. He informed me of a procedure that they had previously performed. This procedure would allow them to put a clamp on the vessel/valve and stop the leaking. However, this was a temporary procedure. This procedure would temporarily protect her lungs. They would later have to go back to remove the clamp and fix her heart when she got older.

We scheduled the appointment for her to come in for the operation at nine months old. My baby would have a heart operation.

I didn't trust the system. I had no idea how advanced the heart doctors were. I was at a loss. I trusted in God. I thanked God that I was finally informed of the situation. I felt confused and worried.

They reassured me that they had performed this procedure many times successfully. They said, "There was much hope for her operation to be successful."

I took her home. You would think I had been selfish about others taking care of her previously. Now, I was the guardian angel.

This information was not what I anticipated when I went to bring my baby home.

This was not a good day for me.

CHAPTER 24

I took my baby home finally. I had scheduled for my Wonie to be operated at a time that would not interfere with my education.

I had now missed graduating in 1968. Too much lost time for me to catch up. It is now the end of June, now summer. I was to go to summer school. I missed graduating by failing two classes. I was determined to pass them in summer school. However, I didn't go to summer school. I went to work instead.

I went back to Hartford High School during the summer and registered for the next year. I would get whatever subjects that I needed to graduate. I was determined to wait until 1969 to graduate onstage. I have worked too hard not to graduate onstage. I could wait for them to hand me my diploma in my hand. I did not want to receive it in the mail.

I now had gotten a job working for the tax department again for the summer. The job would allow me to work part-time while my daughter was being hospitalized, so it will be work and then to the hospital. This will be once she goes into the hospital. Until then, I will work full-time.

The day came for my baby to be admitted to the hospital for her operation. They processed her and assigned her to a room. She was to have open-heart surgery on the next morning. I stayed and put her to sleep before going home.

I left her in the hospital and proceeded to go home. I could not eat. I had trouble sleeping. I woke up after a restless night. I arose early in the morning and went to the hospital. I arrived just as they were preparing to medicate her. I held her and kissed her up. I walked with her down the hallway to the operating room. I cried when they took her through the door and left me standing outside the door.

CHAPTER 25

The operation lasted six hours. I prayed and read a book off tearstained pages. They came out several times to inform me that things were going good. They offered me refreshments. I took coffee only.

Finally, they came out and said the operation was completed. They said she was holding her own, it was successful, and that I could see her in about an hour.

They put her in the intensive care unit or ICU. When I was allowed to see her, I almost fainted. There was a nurse beside her bed. She had multiple tubes attached to her. There were monitoring machines everywhere.

I was not allowed to touch her, only just to look at her. I watched the machine with her heartbeats on it, until they told me that I had to leave.

I kept thinking, *Whatever they did. Her heart is still beating.*

Though, she was still unconscious. She was breathing.

Wonie, remained in intensive care for eight days. She was then sent to the children's ward. She then did not have as many tubes in her. She was fed and medicated through tubes only. She still remained on the heart monitor, and a blood pressure machine was there. She slept most of the time. I still could not hold her, but I could change her diaper and lotion her body.

It was finally time for the stitches to be removed. That is when I found out that they cut my baby from the middle of her little chest. They brought that down to her waist. Then they cut up and around under her little arm and straight up the middle of her back. This was so they could lift that portion to get to her heart. *Oh my god.*

She remained in the hospital for several weeks. I basically lived between work and being in that hospital from morning to night.

Her father still could not visit her in this condition.

She was finally ready to have some more tubes removed. I could not feed her. She was still on intravenous feeding tubes. I still could not hold her, but I could touch her all over her body. I dared not go near the bandages. She was now smiling at me. I give thanks to Jesus.

She smiled when I arrived and was asleep when I left. I sometimes arrived before she awoke and she would light up when she would wake up and saw me. She listened when I talked. I read to her often. This made her happy as well.

CHAPTER 26

I continued this same routine endlessly. One day when I arrived, more tubes were being removed. She could finally eat small portions of real food. I was there to help her eat always. She could now sit up in bed. She was recovering progressively. The bandages finally came off. She was even talking some.

I could now sponge-bathe and dress her. She was now allowed to sleep with her doll. She was healing well and I could now hold her. I was told how to pick her up. I should never pull her up by reaching under her arms. I could reach under one arm and by her bottom. She was not that big so that worked fine. She didn't appear to be in much pain.

They monitored her heart several times a day all the machines were gone. She was now eating with no tubes in her. She had a good appetite. They would now even put her in a playpen. So her mobile skills were coming back rapidly. She was crawling and pulling up to standing position. She walked around holding on to the bars.

She was doing well. She seemed to be back to the way she had been before all this occurred. The two of us played patty-cake and we sang. I read and she pointed at the pictures of what I read about.

The day came for me to take her home after almost a month.

CHAPTER 27

My daughter and I took a cab home. She seemed very happy to be there. She was put down to took a nap, and she said, "My bed."

I was ecstatic when I told her yes.

My mom was very happy it all went so well. My stepdad sat her in the chair with him and smiled. I informed them that she may still be sore inside and instructed them on how to handle and hold her.

Her father Herb didn't know how to act when he did finally show up. She recognized him and reached for him. I then showed him how she was to be picked up. He was fearful so he only held her for a little bit. She was fine with that because she was content in her own bed.

She didn't take long to get back to her old little self. She was talking up a storm. She seemed to be making up for lost time. Or maybe getting out of the way for this baby I will be having in a short time.

She was with me in the mornings in the bathroom. We brushed our teeth. She sat on her potty-chair since the time when she first could sit up. She was trained to go to her potty-chair by the age of ten months. The first time I put her on ruffled panties she was done with wetting her pants. She also walked at ten months. She had very few accidents in her panties, so no more Pampers.

She had a good rest of the summer with me around most of the time. I was still working for the tax department for the rest of the summer. I was able to work some full-time weeks before the summer was over.

We for sure needed the money.

CHAPTER 28

It was now time for me to go back to school. I would only have to take two classes in the morning every day. This would only have to be for half of the year.

So I went to school and straight back home. I fed, bathed, and cared for my baby. At night, I studied with a book in my hand and her across my lap. She went to sleep that way most nights. When I would get up to put her to bed, I would also go.

The time was getting short for me with this latest pregnancy. I wasn't as sick as when I first carried a child inside me. The school system did not know at this point. Therefore, I attended my two classes every day and left unnoticed.

I did not gain much weight. I might have gained twelve pounds at the most. I wore the same jeans into the hospital that I wore when I went home. My baby never moved inside me like the other one had. I sometimes wondered if God had answered my prayers. I even thought, because of no movement, none of this was really true. I asked God for forgiveness for these thoughts of wishful thinking.

I never told the father of this child that I was with child number two. He finally got nerve enough to ask me when I was about seven months. I told him at that time yes. He questioned me about why I had no weight gain. I stated that I had been sick all along. I had not held enough food to gain weight just enough to nourish the baby. The weight gain was obviously enough to sustain us both. I told him I didn't know why.

He decided to tell the people in the neighborhood. He generally told the whole community. The neighborhood started questioning me about my pregnancy. They first tried acting like they were in disbelief. They said I didn't look like it. They confronted me nonetheless. I have always prided myself with finding ways to deal with my own business.

Therefore, I had enough courage and convictions in me to stand up to any and all the questions and the accusations with facts.

I even insinuated that, not only do any of these people have nothing to do with taking care of the child I already have, nor if I should have another, would they be obligated to take care of that one either. That meant the father included. Whatever it looked like to them is all right with me. Whose business was it anyways?

About everything now was taking a toll on me. I am tired, frustrated, and even though I did not look like it, but I was at seven months in my pregnancy.

I had still not told anyone else about this second child that I was carrying. My mother knew, but never confronted me with it. I admitted it to her in my eighth month.

I went to the doctor one time during this pregnancy. I was eight months, and my mom suggested it, so I went. The doctor who examined me wanted to know why I had not come before then. I had no answer. He was concerned and gave me vitamins and a next appointment.

I never got a chance to go back for my next appointment.

CHAPTER 29

My so-called girlfriends and my other associates only looked and wondered.

The look was what sometimes made me want to stop holding my head up. The look even made me want to stop being proud of myself. It was that look that made me just want to lie down and die.

I still never told anyone straight up except for my mom.

My daughter Wonie's birthday was three days away. I was going to get her some cupcakes to celebrate with later on in the day, but I was not feeling too well that day. I went to school and returned home to take a nap. I should have gotten the cupcakes while I was out. I was going to put her down for a nap, and I thought of getting them after my nap.

I awoke to sharp pains. I went to the bathroom. I was bleeding. I called the ambulance after informing my mother of the situation. The ambulance ride seemed long. I hurt badly. Upon arrival to the hospital, I was taken to the emergency room. They wanted to know if I ever had this kind of pain before.

I replied, "Yes, the last time I had a baby."

They examined me and found out that I was in labor. I was very close to delivery. They told me that I didn't appear to be pregnant, but who are they to say? I was rushed down the hall. At that time, they told me that I was too far gone again for local anesthesia. I had dilated and I was X amount of centimeters. They took me into the delivery room and gave me a spinal injection again.

My son Trev was born. He weighed six pounds, nine ounces. He was long, about nineteen inches. The doctor and nurses were surprised that he was that size. They told me that they didn't know where he had been hiding. They cleaned him up and allowed me to hold him. I again checked to see if he had all his fingers and toes. He was moving and crying, and I was too. They didn't have to hit him to make him cry. They said they might have to hit him to make him stop. He was alive and healthy. God was so good to me.

CHAPTER 30

So two days before my daughter turned a year old, my son was born. They were 353 days apart. So they remain the same age for two days as they grew up. I went home a day after her birthday with a very special present. I brought her a brand-new baby brother and cupcakes.

I now had to have her sleep with me and give the baby the crib. She could care less for he was hers as well as mine. She kept saying, "Mine."

I kept saying, "Yep, your baby brother."

Life was not so hard since she was walking and trained. She was helpful. I allowed her to bring me things for him. They ate at the same times. I give him a bottle. I give her a piece of fruit. I give him a bottle. I give her a cookie. I give him a bath in his little tub. I put her in the sink to bathe. I made no difference in the two and they grew up like that.

I had a baby and a one-year-old. Life was different being a mother of two. I loved my children, so I did my best.

CHAPTER 31

I went back to school after three weeks. I had to make up work assignments, but with only two classes, it was not so hard to do. I soon got caught up.

However, I could not work yet. So I went to school and straight back home. I fed, bathed, and took care of two children. At night, I studied with a book in my hand and both of my children across my lap. Both of them went to sleep that way most nights as well. They were asleep head-to-head. When I would get up to put them to bed, I would also go. I was very tired, but I had studied.

I went to work for the post office for their Christmas season. It was not easy. I had to work late, but my mom was good and at home with the kids.

Trev was growing really fast. He kicked the frame of the crib a loose twice. Once down at the bottom he kicked the frame a loose, so the mattress and box spring fell down through the bottom. On the second occasion he kicked, and shook the bars out on the side and they flew off. It was as though he didn't want to be in it. I ended up having to replace it. It could no longer be repaired.

I at that time in my life had worked enough to have money saved in the bank. I only withdrew it when I really needed it. The money I had saved afforded us a comfortable life. I didn't need to ask anyone for much. I bought what we needed. I bought their clothing and their food. My children had their own toys. I paid my mom for babysitting them.

So I purchased my son a newer, sturdier crib. He seemed to like it and did not destroy it.

CHAPTER 32

I worked hard on my school classes. I was able to pass them both by the half of the school year. I passed them even after taking time off to have a new baby. They gave me the credits I had recently earned. This gave me enough credits to graduate in June.

My children are doing well. I took them to their regular doctor's appointments. They are healthy and growing fast. I was well and sort of happy. I had them to keep myself busy, so I bided my time doing what was necessary for the next couple of months.

I knew that God was on my side. A new phase in my life was about to be upon me. I would soon have my high school diploma.

To God be all the glory…

I graduated in June 1969 onstage with two of my own children in the audience.

The End
(To Be Continued)

Volume 3

FOREWORD

She is a native of Connecticut by way of New York. She had been used and abused to no end. She can't blame anyone, but she has suffered by the hands of many others. She was persevering with determination. She moved forward. The way was foggy, but she was determined to do better for herself and her children. She has many family members.

However, most times, it was each man or woman for themselves. She worked hard for whatever she gets. So "Survival of the fittest" was one of her mottos. She doesn't have to beg or borrow, but she gave freely of herself to others. She did this for one reason or another. However, at the end of the day, she turns to the only one who can help her many situations. The almighty one and only God.

The dramas of her life played on.

INTRODUCTION

It seems to Mariea that even when she does her best it is not good enough. She persevered, but how or why is questionable.

Mariea had had a very interesting childhood, just to say the least. She had incurred insurmountable obstacles, yet she pressed on for the higher calling on her life. She now pushes ahead for all the ultimate challenges.

The future has to be better, even though the past had been fulfilling. It had been full of choices and lessons that got her where she is now. She has learned some valuable life lessons. She had suffered some losses. She has endeavored to do better from the lessons she has learned. She can't stop now. No way can she stop with two children. Not after having the second one and her dad coming from New York. He came to see her and his new grandchild. He also came to tell her, not to have any more children from that dude or anyone else unless she got married.

She is a proud, lively, dynamic, phenomenal woman who is strong in her constitution. A motherly woman of color who is determined to achieve a level of greatness befitting a woman of her stature.

S. Aminiah Nialiah, also known as Saundra Foster

CHAPTER 1

Mariea had finished high school. She is almost nineteen. She has two children. She had worked on various jobs to get to this point. She has work ethics.

She had a man Herb, who has not really grown up in many areas. He did not have a job or any real responsibilities, yet he was still around.

She had street sense, book knowledge, and common sense to a degree. She goes to Greater Hartford Community College and applied for night classes. Her mother was still taking care of her children during her absence.

She got accepted to the community college. She took three courses, Accounting I and II and data processing on a college level. She took these three courses one right after the other. She aced all her classes.

She proceeded to apply and get a job at the Bank of America. She would be working in the accounting department. She would be doing the accounting work for this bank.

Her starting date is given to her after her interview and hiring.

The day came for her to start work at the bank. She went to work for her first day. She was given her desk and work assignment. She liked what she is doing. She reiterated to herself that she was good with numbers. So learning their processes came easy. She liked her boss who was a white female named Barb. She made a pretty good amount of money there. She even got to work overtime running the Excel worksheets for the monthly reports.

She saved her money because she felt as though she needed her own apartment.

It was going to be kind of hard to work not living with her mom. Her mom was her main babysitter, yet being in her mom's house with two children, which was already overcrowded, was not correct.

She had to find an apartment soon and move out. She needed her own space for herself and her children.

CHAPTER 2

She talked to her mother Lillie about the thoughts of moving out. Her mother told her if that was what she wanted to do, so be it. Mariea's mother was not pleased with the decision though. She was not sure if that was a good decision at that time. However, she wished her luck in finding something suitable.

She told Herb about her decision to find an apartment. Herb informed her that there was a two-bedroom apartment in the building his sister Plut lived in. He said the rent was not that much.

She found the time to go to talk to Plut about the apartment.

Upon talking to Herb's sister Plut, I told her that even if I could afford the apartment. I would need a sitter for my children. She advised me that she was available for that. She could take care of the children while I worked. She was not employed. I discussed with her how much she would charge me. We agreed upon a price. That, for me, would be very convenient since we would be next-door neighbors.

I found out who the landlord was from her. She gave me his telephone number as well. I called him and he advised me of the terms of the rental.

I agreed upon the terms and we scheduled a time for us to meet.

I met with the landlord and secured the apartment. I paid him what he asked for the apartment.

I had enough money in the bank and a full-time job. So I could afford to pay a month's rent and a security deposit. I could move in on the first of the next month.

CHAPTER 3

I informed my mom of the situation. She seemed happy for me, even though she still didn't really want me to take the children away. She knew she wouldn't be seeing them daily anymore.

I took money out of the bank, and I went furniture shopping. I bought my daughter Wonie a bunk bed that could later have a bed on the top level of it for Trev. This was planning for our future. This was for when he became big enough to sleep in it. At the rate he was growing that wouldn't be too much longer from then.

I purchased a kitchen set. A bedroom set for me. I purchased an upright dresser with several drawers for the children. We did not need a living room set at this time. I made the living room my bedroom. It was actually a one-bedroom apartment which I turned into a two-bedroom apartment with no living room. I could entertain in the kitchen if I had company. The apartment came with a stove and refrigerator, a bathtub, and a shower. I got towels, wash clothes, bed linen, dishes, silverware, pots, and pans.

I bought a scrub board. This scrub board would do until I could afford a washing machine.

I packed up our things we had in my mom's house. I didn't need a moving truck. A girlfriend of mine offered to help me. We were able, when moving day came, to put all our stuff in her car.

Moving day came. I moved to Homestead Avenue.

I had the furniture delivered to my third-floor apartment. I brought all the things I had purchased as well. There was enough room for it in my girlfriend's car.

My girlfriend stayed and helped me to arrange my apartment. This was my first apartment. This was my own space to do what I wanted to do in it. It was a long time coming.

My girlfriend liked the apartment. She then took me to the grocery store. When we got the food, she took me to pick up my children. I paid her and she tried not to take it. I got out and left it on the seat. She cursed me and I laughed. She earned it and I could afford it. I was grateful for her assistance.

Needless to say, I had no other assistance except for my siblings. My mom and stepdad were sad to see me move out. My siblings were really sad yet they were happy for me and their selves because I had my space. They would have more space. They could come over or stay over whenever they wanted to.

We loved each other so much, but without me in Bellevue Square, they really had to be more careful than normal. They had to remember all the little things that I had taught them about survival of the fittest.

CHAPTER 4

I got settled into my first apartment. I had bought Trev a playpen. I put Trev into the playpen, while Wonie explored the apartment. Trev started calling for her. I put her into the playpen with him.

I started to put food up and prepared their dinner. We ate dinner, and I proceeded to get them ready for bed.

There was a knock on the door. It was Herb. He checked the apartment and said I did well. I said my thanks. He asked what I was cooking, and I offered him a plate of food. I had not as of yet learned how to cook for one and a half. So I had plenty enough to offer him a plate.

While he was eating, he asked if I had made him a key. I laughed while stating that he had not found the time to help me to move in. He stated that he was busy and actually he forgot.

I said, "However, when you got finished with your business you remembered to come over here." I then stated, "You only get keys when you pay the rent."

He never paid the rent and he never got a key. He would have to leave when we left. He could only come over after I arrived in the late afternoons. He didn't like it, but he didn't ever pay the bills either.

He really liked my bedroom furniture. He wanted to know if he could spend the night. I was not shocked, so I said "Of course."

CHAPTER 5

I grew accustomed to coming home to my new apartment. I loved picking up my children in the afternoons once I had gone back to work. They were always happy to see me.

I have started to get comfortable in my space. I soon learned that I had forgotten to get a broom, mop, and dustpan. I would have to pick them up on tomorrow before coming in from work. I really liked my first apartment, even though it was on the third floor. It was not a problem until I had to go up and down those stairs with groceries. Wonie could climb up and down the stairs by herself. I got my exercise carrying Trev up and down them though.

I took the cab to the grocery store and I got fresh veggies from my relatives. They were fresh right out of their garden that very same day. They called and asked if I wanted them, and I went to retrieve them.

I also took the cab to the Laundromat now to do my heavy laundry. I washed the light loads in the tub with the scrub board. I hung them on the clothesline off the back porch to dry.

My apartment is clean, neat, and orderly. I enjoyed cooking many different meals. I cooked some of the meals I learned how to cook from my cooking classes in school. I also prepared the meals that my grandma, grandpa, mom, aunts, and dad taught me to cook. I always kept cooked food in my apartment. I kept just enough money out of the bank for what I needed from week to week. Therefore, I am doing okay on my own.

I think that I am grown now.

CHAPTER 6

Okay, now it was time to go back to work. I had taken a week off. I realized that things were working out well with the sitter. She was their aunt, so I was relieved in the evenings to bring the kids across the hall. I would cook, feed them, and put them to bed.

I would usually read. I kept a *Webster's Pocket Dictionary* in my purse for words that I was unfamiliar with. I kept building on my vocabulary.

The job at the bank was very rewarding. I learned a lot. My boss had gotten her masters online. She tried to talk me into doing some online classes. I never did.

I had worked at the bank for about a year now.

I found out that the post office was hiring for the summer. I found the time to apply during one of my lunch hours. The bank was on Constitution Plaza and the post office was on High Street.

I took the postal test. I scored pretty high in the nineties.

I was put up near the top of the hiring list because I had work experience as well with them. That was from the Christmas work I had done.

The hours were different, from 3:00 p.m. to 11:00 p.m., so I asked the sitter if she could accommodate me. She said yes.

I received notification from the post office with a start date.

I soon left the bank and went to work for the post office for that summer.

CHAPTER 7

My children were growing nicely. I took the time to take them to all their doctor appointments. They received all their shots on time. I paid extra attention to Wonie because of her heart defect. She went to the heart doctors regularly as well. They were healthy, happy growing children.

When Trev turned about nine months, he started to try to walk. That's when I noticed that both of his feet were turned at the ankles in the same direction. When he would try to take a step, the foot that followed would knock him down.

Really now, this nine-month notification gave me flashbacks. I received Wonie's diagnosis at this time in her life, now this. I mentioned this when I took him to his clinic appointment. They referred me to a specialist at the children's hospital. I made an appointment there and took him to see the doctors there for this.

They diagnosed him with a fibrous dysplasia which my mom had in her arm. However, being that he was so young, it could be corrected without an operation. He could wear a foot brace on his shoes to sleep in at night.

I didn't have a lot of extra money. I had two children to feed and clothe. This doctor was talking about me buying a new pair of shoes to destroy as far as regular usage was concerned.

You can destroy the shoes, I was thinking. Just say you can fix his ankles. Say that they can be turned around.

They said that as he grows, this will turn his ankles into the correct positions. Since he was sleeping in them and he would do his most growing at night. I trusted that theory.

I told his father just so he would know. He didn't have a solution as to how we could get an extra pair of shoes for him.

CHAPTER 8

It was rent time. The light bill was due.

I was making good money this summer, but I was on a budget. I had to have money in the bank just in case anything happened.

Both of my children needed new shoes. There was no way that I could get around it. I purchased Wonie a new pair of shoes. I had to buy one pair for Trev and bring them to the doctor for him to put a brace on. He was to sleep in this brace each and every night. He slept on his back with his feet stretched out with those shoes on. He would sometimes have them straight up in the air while he slept on his back.

His regular walking shoes would have to wait since he had to have his feet straightened first anyway.

I could put the money back in the bank later.

During this time, my son overcame his own little dilemma. He was determined to overcome. Trev would want to get out of the playpen to try to keep up with Wonie. I put him on the floor.

I would watch him pull up like he did in the playpen. He would then get his balance. I watched him fall and get back up. Then I watched him take a step and only bring the other foot up close to the one in front. He would then move the front foot before moving the back foot. He would lose his balance and fall. He would fall often and get right back up.

He taught himself to walk like that at ten months of age. He wore the shoes to bed for eight weeks and his ankles were straightened out. They grew straight because of the shoe braces. I bought him good Stride Rite shoes to support his ankles and we had no more problems in that area.

My son was also trained to use the toilet at ten months. He was big and strong for my little baby boy.

He no longer had to go to regular-scheduled doctor appointments for his ankles. He was found to be healed. His ankles all straightened out.

I am a proud mother to have trained and walking children at such a tender age of ten months.

I am proud of them.

CHAPTER 9

It was August and the post office put up signs saying that they were going to be giving tests for part-time regulars.

I signed up for the test. I received a letter telling me the times of the testing schedules. I called and I got scheduled for the test. I went to take the four-hour test. This test was in categories. It was challenging. It was hard. It was long.

I received another letter from the post office. I passed this test as well with a ninety-two. I got hired to start in September after the summer session was over. I was so happy.

Summer is coming to an end and I had received notification of my start date. I will be a part-time regular in the US Postal Service.

September came and I went to fill out my entry papers. I started to work on the next Monday. I was working six days a week. My day off will be on Thursdays. I would still be working the second shift from 3:00 p.m. to 11:30 p.m.

CHAPTER 10

My first day of work at the post office again is here. I am overjoyed. Everyone was not so happy for me. My family thought that was great. My sitter did not mind getting the extra pay. My friends were pleased because several of them were afforded the same opportunity. So I would be new but not alone on the new job.

However, Herb didn't think too kindly of the prospect.

Now we lived on Homestead Avenue and the post office was on High Street. It wasn't too far. Since I lived in the first apartment from the corner of Garden Street next to the tire shop. Therefore, I just had to walk to the corner, cross Garden Street to get to Walnut Street. I would go across the railroad tracks, straight, all the way up Walnut Street to High Street. Then I would have to turn right on High Street and go two building down and I would be there.

Therefore, I was told by Herb, that I could not accept any rides home at almost midnight. Herb said this to me.

I said, "Okay, right."

I started to work on my appointed day. I liked being assigned to a specific area to sort mail. This was unlike the summer sessions. In the summer, you went wherever you were needed. You would never know beforehand where you would be working on any given day.

At the end of most nights, I would be offered a ride by males and females. I always declined. I would often say I needed to walk after sitting most of my shift at work. Therefore, I walked home alone in the dark of night, every night. I carried a rug cutter which I had been carrying since fishing days. I stayed alert, even though I was tired. I was somewhat afraid, but I prayed every step of the way.

It seemed as though Herb would be sitting in the window of his sister's apartment awaiting my arrival. Yet he never came to meet me and walk with me ever. I never thought much about it. I was tired. I worked hard and long. So it didn't matter much. I was making my own way.

I was coming home to get my children. I couldn't wait to put my children in their own beds.

However, one particular night, it was storming outside when we got off work. I was offered a ride and I refused. I was persuaded though mostly because I was not prepared for such a storm. My friends were very concerned about my well-being.

So I took the ride. I arrived at home and thanked my friend very much.

CHAPTER 11

I entered the building and proceeded upstairs as usual. When I knocked on Plut's door, Herb answered the door. Upon entering, I talked to her about how the evening had gone. She responded that all had gone well. So I started to gather up my children and their belongings. I went in as usual to retrieve my sleeping children.

Herb followed me around as I did this. He then started asking me questions. He kept following me around her apartment as he talked. I continued to gather the kids and their stuff. He didn't lift a hand or a thing to carry.

Wonie woke up so she could walk across the hall. I picked Trev up to carry him. He remained asleep.

By the time I got to the door to leave, after thanking her for keeping my children, she walked me to the door to say good night.

Herb had started to get loud now because I was not feeding into his conversation. I didn't even answer him once. He was now asking me who brought me home. I told him a friend and nothing more. He wanted to know if it was a male or female. I didn't answer. He continued to say things.

He then said, "Didn't I tell you not to accept any rides from anyone?"

I didn't answer.

I opened the door of her apartment to leave and he shoved me into the hallway. His sister tried to talk to him, but he didn't listen. I proceeded to usher Wonie verbally to go to our door, which I had left ajar. I started walking around the railing of the stairs to pass by the stairwell to enter into my apartment. He shoved me again.

I reached the end of the railing. I am now standing at the top of the stairs. My doorway was to the left of me. He then proceeded to shove me again. I went falling down the flight of stairs. I ball up as I am falling down because I had Trev in my arms. I feared for my child, not for myself. Trev woke up and started screaming. Herb's sister was now screaming at him.

I regained my composure at the bottom of the stairs. I look at my baby who appeared to be okay.

I climb the flight of stairs with my baby still in my arms screaming. Wonie was at the top of the stairs screaming. The neighbors on the second floor opened their doors. They asked if I was okay. I said yes. I reached the top of the stairs. I entered my apartment. He followed before I can close the door. I comforted my son while checking to see if he was all right. I put my baby down in his crib. I then comforted Wonie and put her to bed.

Herb, after pushing me down the stairs, was still running his mouth. I go into the kitchen. He followed, still running his mouth even louder. My children are terrified.

I proceed to get on the phone in the kitchen to called a cab. I can't deal with this any longer. He snatched the phone out of my hand. He was demanding me to tell him who brought me home. He shoved me again, and I landed over by the stove. I always leave my cast-iron skillet on the stove. He attempted to hit me, but I grabbed the skillet and hit him first. He fell down on the floor. He was bleeding from the side of his face and from the side of his head.

I stepped over him lying there on the kitchen floor with his head bleeding. He wasn't talking anymore.

CHAPTER 12

I then called a cab. I got my children fully dressed to leave and go out into a storm. The storm outside was not like this storm inside. I grabbed a few other things for them and put them in a bag. I looked out of the window, and the cab was not there.

When I returned to the kitchen, Herb was still trying to get up off the floor. He asked for something to put on his bleeding spots. I asked him to leave and get something from his sister.

I had again picked up that cast-iron skillet. It was in my hand again.

He left.

I gathered the items for me and my children. I called and talked to my mother while waiting for the cab. She asked if I was okay. No, I wasn't okay, but I could no longer bother her with my burdens. She told me to come home.

The cab came and blew the horn for us to come down. I proceeded out of my house with caution. I talked Wonie down the stairs. Trev was once again in my arms. We made it to the cab. I put the kids down in the cab and went back upstairs and got our things.

The ride was just long enough for me to calm all the way down. We were safe for the time being. There was no need for me to make my mother worry any more than she already was.

I was on my way back home to Bellevue Square.

CHAPTER 13

My mom welcomed us at the door. She took sleeping Trev out of my arms after hugging me up. I went back to the cab and retrieved our belongings. I thanked the cab driver and paid him with a tip.

My mother now had her two adopted sons living with her. These were the two sons whose mother was unfit to raise them. So my mom and her big heart had now adopted them.

I only thought it was crowded in her house when I moved out. Now, it was unlivable, but I was glad to be there. I believed that part of my feeling this way was because I had gotten used to my own space. So I was very uncomfortable here not having any space. My children and I slept on the couch.

Herb would call and come by. I had no conversation for him. This went on for days. The years of abuse finally became my life reality. I finally made up my mind. There would be no more of that. I was not going back to him. I was not going back to that. I was not going back to his "I am so sorry" excuses.

"You pushed me down a flight of stairs with your son in my arms. How can you not know that was wrong? How can you think that sorry could take that away?"

I questioned myself for being so foolish in the past. I had been so very foolish, that he thought it would always be that way. He thought that my life revolved around him. I now really realized that it never had.

CHAPTER 14

I stayed at my mother's house for a week. I talked to a few friends about my situation. They were sympathetic and asked if they could help in any way. I told them, "Thanks, but this was for me to work out."

I went to work and came back and tried to find peace every day.

I finally took my sister back to my apartment with me. I was only going back to the apartment because we needed some things from it. I was confused about my future. I only knew it would not repeat my past with Herb. When we arrived at the apartment, I was terrified by something in the kitchen on the floor under the sink. It happened to be a bat. A live bat. I could see it breathing. *Oh my god.*

My sister, who is naturally scared of everything, was not frightened. She got my baseball bat. She beat the bat to death with that baseball bat. She swept it up and threw it off the back porch. I was shocked by her courage. I questioned her about it. She said that I had always been there for her and that was the least she could do. I was baffled and hugged her up. It was just the knowing that she could step up in that fashion just for me. This made me know she was going to be okay. She was already okay without me.

I was not okay. I could not imagine living in that apartment where a bat or bats could get into. So I came to some conclusions at that point. I made up my mind that I was moving out of that apartment. I was going where. I hadn't decided yet.

I spoke to Plut about my circumstances. She tried to convince me to stay in the apartment. I thanked her for all she had done and said my goodbye.

I gathered up more of my children and my own belongings. I took food out of the refrigerator. I took canned goods out of the pantry. I called us a cab because there was too much stuff for us to walk back to the house with.

The cab came. My sister and I went back to my mom's house.

CHAPTER 15

I kept being harassed by Herb with the "come back to me" call. I would only listen then hang up. I had no energy for that conversation.

I made up my mind to give up the apartment and to quit my job.

My family thought I was a little crazy. I knew that I was tired of him and didn't need to be in close proximity of him. I gave up trying to make them understand. They didn't have to live with him or his aggressions. I could not allow him to rule me by any means necessary, especially when he footed not one bill, and I had many.

I informed a few friends at work that I was quitting and moving to New York. They invited me to party with them before I left.

We left work one weekend night, and I went to the party with them. On the way, we smoked some weed and drank some beer. The chick next to me was very close to me. I didn't think much of it since there were three of us in the back seat. When we arrived at the party, it was a nice loft apartment. The music sounded really good. However, I was looking around checking the place and the people out. It seemed like a strange situation. There were some males there with other males. There were a lot of females. They were drinking and drugging. They were dancing with each other. They were hugging and kissing each other. It didn't take long to find out even though I had not suspected. My friends were gay.

They didn't hit on me. I didn't dance with them, but they did ask me to. I just had not known that they were what they were. I was not the one. I didn't go that way with another woman.

To each his own, but that was not for me. We partied, and they took me home to my mom's house.

I had given my job a two weeks' notice reluctantly.

CHAPTER 16

I gave my notice to my landlord. I lost my security deposit since I gave him short notice. He would otherwise lose money. I understood his point.

So I lost a little money to gain a little sanity, I thought.

I could not live in my mother's house with all those people. It was too close to Herb and I was sick and too tired of being bothered by his presence. I decided to go to my dad's house in New York. So I called him and explained my situation. He asked if I was sure that I wanted to give up all I had worked so hard to get and come there. He told me that he would never deny me if that was my decision.

I went back to my apartment. I rented a U-Haul truck. I got a few friends, I packed my belongings up, they loaded the truck, and I put my things into storage the day I quit my job.

I made reservations with Greyhound. My mom was in despair. She didn't want me to move to New York. However, she gave me her blessings and many hugs.

I left Hartford with two children heading for my dad's house in New York. I left with bare necessities only. I had money so I could buy whatever else we needed.

I arrived in New York at Port Authority of New Jersey and New York with baggage and two children. I put my baggage into a locker except for what I could carry with my baby. We took the subway and my dad picked us up at the stop. I informed him of the locker. He replied that he would go there and pick up my things on the next day.

He hugged and kissed me and the kids. We proceeded to go to his house after stopping at the grocery store.

I finally get to my dad's house.

CHAPTER 17

I had no idea what I was thinking when I decided to make this move. I could not have thought this move through thoroughly, but here I am.

My dad and my stepmom have a house full already. He had family and friends in attendance right now. He had people and cats. I don't care much for cats. They jump up on the couch and I jump up off the couch. I would never hold one in my lap or pet one for that matter. He had family and friends living in the house and in the basement. There was always someone there. How could I have forgotten?

I am glad to be away from Hartford, but being here was totally different to me when I was alone. Now, I had to try to make this home with and for my children. I am told where to put my things. My family and some of my friends were glad to see me and the kids. I felt very welcome. I tried to get settled in.

There was liquor and drugs around everywhere. We could smoke weed in the house, out on the front porch, or in the backyard. There was even weed growing in the garden. I never asked whose it was.

I had been smoking cigarettes since I was thirteen and they were thirty-five cents a pack. My mom found out and questioned me about it. She gave me permission as long as I would buy my own. She would not support my habit since she did not smoke.

This is not what I imagined being here would be like. I guess there was no imagination. I just needed to get away from a situation. However, I have now created a new and different situation for myself. There was a houseful of children. Some lived there and others were with their visiting parents. So my children fit right in. I fed my children. I bathed my children and put them to bed. We slept in a bed together. We were now used to that from the couch at my mom's house.

I didn't have to get up to go to work, so we slept late. I had no job to go to. For right now, my children were my only job. I got up dressed and fed my kids. I then walked across the street from the house and took them to the park. This is where I pondered over my situation for most of the day.

I have to be here right now. I have nowhere else to go. It is going to all work out somehow for my good. God willing.

CHAPTER 18

I had to decide what my next moves were going to be. I wasn't doing much except taking care of my kids. I drank some and smoked some weed. This was trying to be my daily dues.

I looked in the newspaper and found a few job prospects. After the first few days, I made calls and beat the pavement. There was no problem leaving the kids with their grandparents. They seemed to always have somebody's kids around anyways.

I had no luck finding a job that week. I could have taken a job cleaning offices. However, I wasn't used to cleaning offices. I had worked in offices, but not to clean them. That was not for me. I am not trying to go backward just for survival tactics. I still had some money in the bank so I was holding on.

So I fell into the nothingness of getting high and doing nothing. I played cards from time to time. We went out to party on the weekends. We watched movies during the week. They always had some get high. I indulged some but not too much. I was spending money and not making any. I refused to be a part of a lot of their behavior because not all of them had money and they knew that I did. My money was not for the get high stuff.

We had some of our cousins to come from Chicago. My brother had given me a marijuana bud. I stuck it in my purse. I really didn't want to share it. We were all sitting on the front steps just enjoying the weather and each other. My cousins decided to go across the street to smoke in their van. I was invited, and I went. I had no idea what they were smoking in the back of the van. I was smoking weed, listening to the music and enjoying their company.

Then there was a loud knock on the window. The police were knocking on the window and the door on both sides of the van. They proceeded to raid the van, asking us all to get out. I got out smiling as the others were getting arrested for smoking crack. Then they came to me. They searched my purse and handcuffed me for possession of that bud of weed. I had forgotten all about it. Therefore, I was arrested just like the others. I was arrested with my children standing across the street with my parents looking.

The arresting officers had me in the paddy wagon for hours. They kept driving down into alleys and parking and then going to Dunkin' Donuts. I feared that they would do something to me while they kept parking in these dark alleys. I found out later that they were holding off bringing me in to be processed. That was so I would have less time in a cell before they brought me in front of a judge.

I was finally brought to the police station at the crack of dawn. I was fingerprinted, mug shots were taken, and I was put into a cell. Once in the cell, this chick decided to take my blanket off the only cot that was free. I walked across the room and I took it back and went to that free cot. I then told her not to F with me. She stood off looking at me. I then told her not to even think about it. She then sat down on her cot and left me alone.

I was in jail and furiously afraid, but not of her.

I was brought before the judge. He said to me, as a first offender, he would put me on probation for a year. He said that if I was good for five years, it would fall off my record. I was then dismissed. I left walking away from there as fast as I could. My dad had left home and came to get me. My dad picked me up somewhere down the street. I refused to stand outside and wait. I needed to get as far away from there as possible.

My dad took me back to the house. I returned to my dad's house to find out that I was missing money out of my pocketbook. I later found out that it was taken by one of my kids. I didn't really care. All that I cared about right then was being free.

CHAPTER 19

I went through the motions like nothing had happened to me. I was mentally disturbed though. This was not the life I had envisioned.

I helped my dad in his garden. I helped with the cleaning of the fresh veggies. I picked fruit from his trees. They all, especially my children, got a kick out of seeing me climb the trees or pick grapes from his vines. My kids and I ate fresh fruit all the time. I didn't have to cook much. My dad did the most of the cooking. So we ate very well.

I got a Sunday paper and tried the job hunt again. That was also to no avail. I had never had a problem finding a job. This was all new to me. Now, I was spending money and not making any. This was not what I do. I have never functioned like I am functioning now.

This is not working out the way I planned the plan that I didn't plan.

My life was not pleasing to me. I still am not able to find a job. I am not doing anything productive. I don't want to raise my children in New York. I now knew that the pace was not what I wanted for them or me. I am very dissatisfied these days.

September was almost over, and my children would have birthdays coming up soon. I decided to go back to Connecticut. I could not continue going on the way I was going.

I didn't want to fit into this mold. I had enough of this way of life.

I talked to my dad, and he said okay to my decision. I called my mom and she said okay with her as well. It was my choice where I wanted to live and what I wanted to do. They all understood.

I partied that weekend with family and friends. I said my goodbyes until the next time. I packed my stuff and left the beginning of the week.

My dad drove me to Port Authority. We said our so longs. He never says goodbye.

I boarded the bus. All three of us sat in the two seats. They were excited to be going to see Grandma Lillie. We ate the sandwiches I had prepared. They drank milk and we slept through the ride.

We arrived at the Greyhound Bus terminal. I got a cab and we took the last ride back to Bellevue Square.

I would be at home again, Bellevue Square in Hartford, Connecticut.

CHAPTER 20

My mom, stepfather, and siblings were very glad to see me and the kids. The kids missed them as well. It was almost great to be back. I never saw that coming. It was calming, not chaotic. There was almost some order to it. I almost let my guard down in the first few seconds of my being back home. It was like a total transition. Being back in Hartford versus being in New York with two kids was so very different. I knew I had made the right decision to come back now. I had not been gone that long. It was just long enough for me to get a grip on myself.

You see, my mom lived in a five-room apartment. My dad had three floors and a basement. Both of them have a lot of visitors. However, you could never fit the amount of people living or visiting in my father's house into my mom's house at one time. It now almost feels comfortable to be back at my mother's house.

I talked to my mom a long time about what my next moves would be. I needed a job and an apartment. She suggested I go to the Housing Authority and apply for an apartment in the projects. I had never thought about an apartment there. I always thought about getting out of there. Yet the rents were cheap and she was there so I would have a sitter close by.

The kids played with my parents and my siblings. I fed them, bathed them, and put them down to sleep.

I could finally sit down, think, and breathe now.

There was only a week to go to my children's birthdays. So I thought about what one would do for a one- and two-year-old. It would not be very much. Their birthdays are on Friday and Sunday. Therefore, I would celebrate on Saturday of the next week. They would both be one-year-olds for two days. Then Wonie would turn two. For years, they said that they were twins for two days. They were that close. She looked out for him all the time. If he fell, she would help him up. He was her brother by all means. She was possessive. He belonged to her.

CHAPTER 21

I arose the next morning to feed the kids and set out to look for a job and an apartment. I was not wasting any more time.

I got lucky with the Housing Authority. I had gone there first. I informed them that I was in transition between jobs. They told me that they had a few vacant apartments. I was able to select which one I would be interested in. I had money enough in my bank account for the first few months' rent. I had a good track record of employment. So they gave me an apartment to move into in two weeks. I was to notify them as soon as I became employed. I was pleased. It would literally be right across the yard from my parents' house.

I went downtown and filled out several applications for jobs. I felt good about myself. I had not had that feeling for quite some time now with my life in limbo.

I had not told many that I was home, but I wasn't hiding either. I returned to the house and took my kids to the playground. The secret was out. I ran into many friends who thought I was on one of my New York vacations. It was too soon that Herb discovered my presence back in town. Some of his family had been at the playground.

Herb stopped by the house. He wanted to see the kids. They visited. I watched television. I didn't have any conversation for him. He kept trying to talk to me to no avail. I finally fed the kids and started to get them ready for bed. He didn't catch the hint until I asked my mom if she would watch the kids for a few hours. She replied yes. Herb asked me where I was off to, I asked him why. He said that he came to visit, and I was leaving.

I said, "You visited the kids and they are gone to bed."

He got upset but he left.

I left shortly afterward. I visited a friend who told me about a job prospect. I talked to her about my life situation. She offered me some good advice. I stayed about an hour and went back home. It was kind of good being back on more familiar territory.

CHAPTER 22

I arose early the next day. I prepared breakfast for my kids and siblings before they went to school. I ate a little. I was on another mission.

I left the house to go back downtown. This time, I went to city hall. This was where my friend Pat said that they were doing some hiring.

Now I still visit her occasionally. We are still friends. This is the friend whose house I had gotten raped in.

When I arrived at city hall, they had a lot of job postings on the walls. I found the one my friend had suggested. It was with the Department of Housing. They needed to hire people for the position of relocation aides. So I went into the room that was noted on the posting. I filled out an application. I had good work experiences so that was easy. I got an interview.

They explained that there were parts of Hartford that were sighted for redevelopment. They needed relocation aides to help. The aides would be working in an office setting. They would have a workload of clients in various areas. The aides would have to go out to those areas. They would have to visit the people who were being displaced. They would have to explain the redevelopment situation. The aides would have to help those people find apartments. They would also set up moving dates and the movers for the displaced clients. It all sounded good. They took my application and told me that I would hear from them within the next few weeks.

I went back home feeling like I might have an apartment and a job very soon.

CHAPTER 23

It is now Friday. My baby Trev turned a year old. I told him so. Wonie and I put up one finger, and so did he.

I fed them pancakes, and we sang "Happy Birthday" to him. They were both giggling with me. I dressed them and I got dressed to go out.

I had a very productive week. I was feeling good about myself. I proceeded to take them with me to the five-and-ten cent store. I bought a few decorations, ice cream, cake mix, and frosting. I told the little kids in the building about the party. I also told some of the other kids in the general area. I told the parents to bring the kids over on tomorrow at three o'clock. We then returned to the house.

I put the things I had bought up and took the kids back outside. I sat on the outside bench, and I let them play in the dirt. I checked my schedule to see when they had doctor's appointments while they played. They had not missed any appointments. They did have a few appointments coming up soon.

I took them in, cleaned them up, and fed them lunch. We had an uneventful afternoon. They played outside again. I cleaned them up again and put them into their pajamas. They fell asleep in my lap while I watched TV.

I informed the kids' father that evening about the party I was having by phone. He had forgotten that it was Trev's birthday and blamed it on me. *Duh*.

CHAPTER 24

It was now Saturday morning. I fixed us all breakfast.

My siblings were so excited they wanted to start decorating. I told them it was too early and we didn't have that much to do. I said we should make the cake. They all crowded around the table happy to do that.

My siblings got the eggs, butter, and pans while I got the bowl and turned on the stove. My babies just watched with glee.

When the cake went into the oven, they all ate out of the bowl and had cake faces.

I suggested we get cleaned up for the day while the cake cooks. They thought that was a good idea. I cleaned and dressed my kids. My siblings did the same.

The cake was done. I informed them that a bunch of little kids would come for the party. So we made little sandwiches. I put some candy in some bowls. We put up the little decorations I had bought. They handed me the tape while I stood on the chair.

We gathered again around the table, and I frosted the cake. They put out paper plates, spoons and folded napkins. Then I made punch and gave them sandwiches and punch for lunch. The day was a happy one so far for all.

CHAPTER 25

I had bought Wonie a new dress. I finally bought Trev his Stride Rite shoes. These would be their birthday presents along with a wagon and a black Raggedy Ann doll.

The time came for the party. People started knocking on the door. It was my brother's job to answer the door and let people in.

We had about ten children and six or seven grown-ups. I played music and they danced and played together. My children were glad to have so much company. For them, it was like being in New York.

Their father came by. He stayed for a little while. He stayed long enough to ask if he could take Wonie over his mother's house on tomorrow. He wanted only Wonie. He didn't think he could take them both at the same time. I agreed. I informed him that I would be picking her up about three o'clock. He said okay.

The day went by. They ate sandwiches, cake, and ice cream. We opened presents. Trev and Wonie were delighted. Wonie wanted to put her dress on, but I told her tomorrow. Trev rode people in his wagon after he put on his new shoes. Most of the other gifts were cars, books, and gift cards. They all enjoyed themselves. The party was over at 5:00 p.m. I had enough of the running, screaming and crying.

I thanked everyone and said our goodbyes. What a day. A birthday party for one-, two-, three-, and four-year-olds is not funny. The kids were all happy, running, screaming, and crying.

CHAPTER 26

Sunday was now Wonie's birthday. We ate breakfast, sang, and put up two fingers. My mother thought all this was funny because it was me and not her. She let me just handle all of it.

I dressed the kids. I put Wonie in her new dress. Trev got dressed and we put on his new shoes.

Their father came and took Wonie, and Trev cried. I proceeded to take Trev to visit with my aunt Mae. We had a good day, and I pulled him in his wagon. So he only missed Wonie for a minute.

Now I was having a good day. I had purchased myself a light and dark pleather coat. I thought I looked good. I felt good in it.

At around 2:30 p.m., I asked one of my cousins to give me a ride to go get Wonie.

Herb's mother had moved out of the project to Oakland Terrace into a house by now.

Upon arrival, I spoke to everyone. I then asked for Herb. Wonie came running to me when she heard my voice. Trev was glad to see her.

When I spoke to Mrs. J, Herb's mother, she spoke. She then said, "Your coat is nice, but Renee has a real leather coat like that."

Now Renee must have been another one of Herb's ladies. I replied, "If your son helped me financially with his two children, maybe I could afford a real leather coat as well."

She said she meant no harm. One of her children said something to her. I proceeded to get Wonie ready to leave while Trev gave his grandma a kiss.

Before I left, I told her that her house was nice.

She said, "Thanks I have enough room now."

I said, "I am very happy for you."

Now I always respect my elders. So I went down the stairs praying for forgiveness and praying for her.

I also thought, *Forgive me, Lord, but the truth hurts.* I guessed you could have seen that on my face and on hers.

I don't think I ever went back over there.

CHAPTER 27

I now have a one-year-old and a two-year-old. I take them to their prospective doctor appointments. Both the primary care units and the heart specialist give my children clean bills of health. The both of them are well and growing as they should. Wonie's heart is pumping strong for a two-year-old.

Trev is a busy little fellow. His brain works faster than his mouth. He does not as yet know how to position his tongue to pronounce words. He gets frustrated with my mom. He acted as though she should understand him. So when he is asking for "coookeee" and she has no idea what he is saying, he sits in the floor quietly and doesn't talk. Therefore, not too many people can understand what he says. Most people think that he is babbling. He has stopped talking so much to other people. If I am not around, he holds his conversations until I am around. Then he blurted out what was on his mind in my absence.

Wonie understood him, and sometimes she talked for him. She shared everything with him. He sometimes pulled on her clothing to get her attention and she gives it to him. I watch, and it amazes me how they communicate.

I sat down, but first he asks for a cookie his way. I gave him the cookie and my attention. I can understand him. I slow him down, and when I repeat words, he repeated them. When I get it, he smiles and hugs me. My son is smart and doesn't yet know how to let it be known to anyone other than me.

CHAPTER 28

I am doing well though I don't check my health as much as I check theirs. I haven't gotten sick in a long while, so I am all right.

I got the job with the city and the apartment. I am on full speed to get the apartment situated before I start my new job.

The apartment they gave me was on the first floor. That made it easy for me to move into it. I have gotten my furniture out of storage. I bought another bunk bed and the staircase to get to the top. There will be no more crib for Trev. Wonie can climb to the top bunk and not fall out of bed with the railing I purchased. I don't have any living room furniture but I glued a tile rug on the floor and bought pillows to put around the wall space. I covered the entire floor. I purchased a stereo. I also purchased a used washing machine. When I got everything done, I went and got my children and my mom. They were pleased to see their own stuff and they knew they were home. Wonie climbed up the ladder to her bed and said, "Like this has got to be mine."

Trev was put on his bed, and he said, "Mine."

I said yes and gave them both a hug. They explored our little apartment, and both found the bathroom soon after.

My mother Lillie was glad to have me living right across the yard from her. She could look out of the window at any time and see the kids playing in the yard.

I made dinner and brought my mom some. My siblings came over and ate with the kids. They were glad to have us so near. Everything in this part of my life seemed to be falling into place.

After dinner, they all went out in the front yard for an hour. My children came in, took bathes, we brushed our teeth, and they went to their new room. They got into their new beds. I tucked them in, said good night, and they soon fell asleep.

I realized that I needed fans in our new apartment. No way could I sleep on the first floor with the windows open. I sat and listened to music for a while, then I closed the windows and the curtains. I slept very peacefully.

I thanked God for making a way for me to start a new chapter. In this life I live.

CHAPTER 29

We got settled in, and things were going smoothly. The children were happily growing up.

I started my new job with the city. We were given a workload. We were assigned to an area of town. We had a class on procedures and guidelines. They teamed us up in sets of two. There would be one with a car and one without. There would also be one that spoke Spanish in each team. We remained in the office for the week. We were getting files and territories set up to go out into the field on next week. The teams worked together on this.

I liked my boss and my coworkers.

We went to work on the next week. We had a short briefing and went out into the field to start the process.

I liked the job with the exception of having to visit the Puerto Rican community. I have a problem with smelling or eating garlic. I would approach a building, and before I could get to the client's apartment, I would get sick and vomit. I explained to my partner what was going on. So we came to an agreement as to how we would handle certain areas of the job. That part of the job worked out for us.

We visited many clients, explaining what was going on and what their incentives were for moving. We found out family size and areas of interest. We sent movers on moving day and visited when clients move. We authorized their payments for being relocated or giving up their living quarters for the city once they relocated as well. The job was very rewarding for the clients and the workers.

Everyone would get paid very well.

The job was on north Main Street. So I could bring the kids across the yard and walk to work and back home in no time. I worked 8:00 a.m. to 4:30 p.m. The benefits and pay were very good. I didn't miss working nights at the post office now. I was able to be home in the evenings for dinner with the kids. I could also fix them breakfast in the mornings before going to work.

CHAPTER 30

The year was going by swiftly. My work days were going well. Many clients were finding suitable housing in nice neighborhoods. Some of the clients were even purchasing homes.

I found out that there was a community organization opening up in Bellevue Square. It would be run by Gwen Reed. This organization would be a two- and three-year-old learning center. This would be for the Bellevue Square Project and the surrounding areas. I immediately registered my children for this center. I informed them during our initial conference that Trev would not be two years old until October. They said that they would overlook that factor because he was trained and they enrolled him for their September sessions.

October came and the children turned two and three years old. They were now going to pre-preschool on a daily basis. I could drop them off before work and pick them up after work. They fed them lunch and a snack. My children loved being there all day with so many other children. They taught them many things. I was in heaven. I had no idea how much they were doing until I was called in to speak with them after a few months.

I took an afternoon off and went for the conference. These were very nice people. They took care of our kids with tender loving care. They taught these babies how to function at such a tender age. They had a lot of stuff going on in the facility. They had a speech therapist as well. The therapist had diagnosed Trev and wanted to work with him. She told me what I already knew, but I listened because she was a specialist. She said he was a very bright two-year-old. He followed directions very well. However, he needed to be taught how to use his tongue to formulate his speech. She could not go any further without my written consent. Oh my god. Look at God. My son was to get help at no cost to me. Of course, I signed the consent form. I thanked them and made a donation for them to buy snacks or lunches for the children.

I gained more that day than the half day's pay that I would lose.

CHAPTER 31

Things were moving in a lot of different directions. I am still working for the city. I still saved some of my money. I kept a bank account. The kids were doing well in school.

I often took them to see their great-grandpa Frank. He only lived a few building away from us, just down the hill. The kids would visit him. They would knock on the door. He would say "Who is it," and Wonie would say "Me." He would open the door. They would enter into his apartment. He would hug them up. He would bounce them on his knees until I would say "Enough," and they were all laughing with so much joy by this time.

This was all before Grandpa fell and broke his hip. He then went to live with my aunt, his eldest daughter. She was the one with the panty ethic. She always wanted to know if yours were clean. We couldn't visit him quite as much then.

My grandpa died shortly afterward at the age of eighty-seven.

I went back to dancing classes at the Artist Collectives. I take African and tap dancing with the adults now. The classes are a diversion from my daily schedule. I am enjoying them.

The kid's father Herb was still around, just not around me.

I ran into several guys that I spent some time with. One guy in particular, Ames, whom I thought I could trust. He was a good lay. I later found out he was addicted to drugs.

One night while I was playing cards, he came over to my mom's house. I talked to him briefly. He wanted to get my key to my apartment. I gave it to him. I thought I could trust him. He later returned it. When I got home, my stereo system was gone. He denied taking it, but my house was not broken into. I fired him and bought a new stereo system.

I sure learn the hard way.

CHAPTER 32

I now hang out with four other young ladies. Two live in the projects I live in.

This friend Bev lived some distance away. Now her mom lives in Harlem, New York. I took the weekend and went with her to see her mother. I told my mom I was going to see my dad. We visited her mom who owned a club. Her mom was also into a lot of other things.

Bev and I did some drugs. We took some acid called "orange sunshine." We walked the streets for hours. We ended up in a male dorm. We had an orgy there. I woke up the next day on the roof of the dorm. We went home. I never did see my dad.

Another one of my friends, named Bren, didn't live too far away from me. She lived on Mahl Avenue. She had a cemetery in back and on the side of her house. I visited her at her house and she visited me. I knew her from the post office. I had worked with her at the post office one of those times I had worked there. We had remained friends. We stayed in contact with each other. I never considered her like the others that I partied with at the post office gay. However, I found out that she went both ways. She would spend the night some times. She would sleep in the bed with me. That was until one night I was taking a bath with the door open. She remarked, that my breasts looked small but nice. I immediately got out of the tub and closed the door. From then on, if she spent the night she would have to make a pallet. She never slept with me again.

Bren and I went to New York once to see a new friend of hers. We went to a Bronx apartment. There were two guys there. I was introduced. I sat in the living room with one of them. She proceeded to go into a bedroom with the other. I heard her scream, a bloodcurdling scream. I ran into the bedroom. I already had my rug cutter out. This guy had set her hair on fire. This was to scare her into doing what he wanted. I grabbed the covers off the bed and put the fire burning her hair out. This guy grabbed at me cursing. I cut him, and we left him bleeding as we fled from that apartment.

I hung out with these ladies often. We were on the wild side. We did most things together, but neither of them had kids yet.

The other two friends I mentioned were not as wild.

CHAPTER 33

I started having rent parties on the weekend, once a month. This is something I got from my mom and her sisters. These four friends of mine were my partners in crime. One of these ladies worked the door. I charged minimal at the door. One of them sold liquor. Another one of these lady friends of mine served as a bouncer. She was kind of large. I handled the food and most of the money.

There were a lot of college students that came to my parties. I always had a houseful of people. I never ran out of food or drinks. I made a lot of money on Friday and Saturday nights. I didn't split the money because I furnished the venue, the liquor, and the food. I paid them salaries. They worked for and with me. We made out very well. The rent got paid with money left over to bank.

Now I had a cousin named Ed who was in the Army. He would come home on some weekends. He would bring home with him Acapulco red and Panama gold weed. He would always have enough for me. I would pay him for his troubles. This weed was so potent that it only took one toke to do the trick. We would sit around the living room and pass one joint. I would tell them to take one toke and pass it on around the room. I would shut down the bar and grill for a few to do this. You would be high by the time it got back to you. I would then go to the bathroom and back to the kitchen.

So the parties were all the way live from Friday evening until about 4:00 a.m. Saturday morning. At that time, I had to put people out. I would say, "Maybe I will see you again tonight."

There would always still be a house full of family members and close friends left in the apartment. I would then proceed to shut off the music. I would go into my bedroom. I would close my bedroom door. I would count my money. I would then put it up and go to bed.

It was always a definite for Saturday night. The house would be full. The money would be made. The fun would be had.

CHAPTER 34

Even though Mariea was into a lot of things she does her best as a mother. In spite of it all, she was raising her children the best way she would know how.

None of her mess goes on in their presence.

Mariea worked, and the children attended school every day. She cooked and kept a clean house. The children are doing very well in school. They are growing and advancing in all areas. They know their ABCs, and they can count to twenty.

My dad, Cal, visited me and the kids. He gave Wonie a dollar. He told her to give Trev half. She thanked him and tore it in half. I had to take it and explain that one was no good without the other half. I allowed her to tape it back together and Trev to watch while I held it. We then took it to the store for them to spend.

Trevor can talk very well now. He talked an awful lot. He was a curious character. He played tricks on his sister and found it to be very funny.

My mom made the mistake of telling him that boys can go to the bathroom anywhere. So not a day goes by that someone doesn't knock on the door to tell me that Trev peed on them. He got to do time-out for that every day.

Trev was now in preschool and Wonie is in kindergarten.

The heart doctor, Dr. Kamiti, has informed Mariea that the time was nearing for Wonie's second heart operation. We scheduled it for late in June of that year.

CHAPTER 35

The job Mariea had with the city was starting to wrap up. The city has relocated most of the people who had lived in the sited redevelopment areas. They have started the demolition destruction of the vacated houses. Home visits to the client's new residences are coming to an end. The end date has been set for our completion of all paperwork.

I secured a job with the Hartford Insurance Company. It was located on Garden Street. I did this before the end date of the city job. I refused to be jobless. I postponed my start date to complete the job with the city.

We completed the relocation efforts. We had an end of work duty farewell party. I enjoyed working with this crew very much. It was a diverse group of individuals. We got the job done. We said our goodbyes as we told stories of what our work had entailed for each of us.

I began work for the Hartford Insurance Company the next week. The insurance work was sort of like the work at the bank. There was always something to do for the many constituents who they serviced. I got my training. I was put on a three-month probation period. I was assigned to a specific area. I got my desk, computer, and all the necessary supplies. I went to work on my new job duties. The day went by with no problems.

CHAPTER 36

I walked to work every day. I always arrive on time. I did the assigned work duties.

The day soon came when my probation ended. I was given a new work assignment. This new assignment would lead me to more money. I was up for the challenge. It went well and I got reassigned again because of it. I was moving right along in this company. I had quite a few friends that I ate lunch with. Things were great for me. I was pleased with myself.

The day came for Wonie to go into the hospital. I had worked long enough to get a week off with pay.

I took Wonie into the hospital for admission. I did my best to explain to her that they were going to fix her heart. She was put in the ward for children. I stayed with her for lunch. She could not eat dinner, and she was not pleased. They started putting tubes into her arms and she was angry with me. She could not have any food and now this. I tried to explain to my five-year-old, but to no avail. She did not want to hear what I had to say. She could not understand why I allowed them to do this to her. I held her until she went to sleep restlessly. I prayed over her, and I left her in the hospital.

CHAPTER 37

I arrived at the hospital at 5:30 a.m. She was awake and still angry with me. I talked to her, but she couldn't talk with the tube down her throat. She cried. I cried and held her.

They took her to the operating room at 6:00 a.m. I sat and drank coffee for hours. They came out and gave me updates. They said that the operation was going well. They finally came out eight hours later. They then said that the operation was a success. I was a little relieved, but I couldn't see her for another hour or two.

They had gone into her chest cavity. They did this by cutting her straight down the middle of her chest. They started from just below her neck and went down to her waist. They had removed the clamp that they put into her at nine months old. This clamp had been to save her lungs from retaining leaking fluids. When they removed the clamp they saw that the hole in her heart was now the size of a fifty-cent piece. They repaired the leaking valve in her heart, closed the hole, and stitched up her chest. She was now in intensive care once more. Hopefully for her, this will be the last time. She has now had two open-heart surgeries. She had one at nine months, and now this one at five years old. My prayers are with and for her right now.

I finally got to look at her through the intensive care window. She had many tubes and a monitor for everything. I felt faint. They gave me a sedative and a chair. I sat here for hours, watching the machines. They finally sent me home.

I visited her every day. Nothing has really changed. On the fourth day, I was able to go into the room. Most of the tubes are out. There were still a lot of monitors in the room and a nurse.

We cried because she was saying, "Mommy, why you letting them hurt me."

I am heartbroken. I am trying to explain to a five-year-old that her heart was broken. I told her that they had to fix it. I could only rub her face, her head, and her arms trying to console her. They finally sedated her, and I had to leave. This went on for many more days.

She was finally sent back to the children's ward. She was still very angry with me. At one point, she would not eat for me. I told her that she would not get better if she didn't eat. I was the villain. I was distraught. I kept coming and staying with her though. She could now feed herself. She was allowed to get out of bed. She still had the heart monitor. I would walk with her up and down the hall.

She was allowed to go home three weeks later. She is strong and defiant. It took a while for her to finally get back to the relationship we once had. Trev was a big help because she refused to let him have me to himself.

Thank God for small miracles.

CHAPTER 38

Things were starting to get back to some kind of normalcy. Mariea was working and enjoying the job. She was hanging out with her girl-friends sometimes, but not wilding so much. She had gone on a few dates. She went out with a man from work and a few others. None of them were what she was looking for, whatever that was.

Wonie was going into the first grade. Her heart was all repaired. She would only have to see the heart doctor twice a year. She was chosen by the Heart Association to be the Heart Princess of the Year. This was for their yearly fund-raising drive. She modeled a little with her crown on. They fed us a nice luncheon.

Trev was going to kindergarten delighted to be going to a real school like his sister.

Mariea met a man named Ron. He started to come around often. The two of them started dating each other regularly. He was good to the kids. He took us all places to eat and otherwise. He was an Army veteran. He worked as a radiator repairman. He bought us things, toys, and books for the kids. He gave me flowers for no rea-son. He soon started spending nights with us. He would drop me off at work before he went to work. The kids didn't seem to mind having him around at all. We kept this up for some time. Then he started talking about me moving out of the projects.

I considered the moving factor. So I decided to move was a good idea. I did move, but to another project. I moved to Bowles Park. The kids were registered for school at Mark Twain. It was a different kind of project. It was like a house apartment connected to another apartment. There were no apartments on top of each other in our building. Some had two floors, but not ours. We were all happy living there.

I had a neighbor who took care of the children until I found out that Wonie had smoked some of her weed. She apologized, but I didn't trust that situation anymore. I then got a cousin of mine to come over in the mornings and send the kids to school and come back when they returned from school. They gave her a fit. One day, I came home from work and she quit. I whipped them for misbehaving. I missed a day of work because of that.

I found another sitter, named Eleanor, that day. She lived in the neighborhood just down the street from us. Her price was affordable. She took care of most of the children in the project. I could drop them off before going to work and pick them up on my return from work. So my kids could walk to school with lots of other kids. When they got to the street to cross to go up the hill to the school, they had a crossing guard. I felt safe with that.

The kids were allowed to have dogs and cats in this apartment. Ron liked that idea. Therefore, we bred Doberman pinschers and cats. We sold a lot of dogs and cats.

I went to driving school. I needed transportation. I used some of my savings to buy myself a car.

CHAPTER 39

Things were still going well. I got pregnant with my third child.

This pregnancy was different from the other two. I was not so sick. I think maybe I was taking better care of myself. The other two kids were excited to know they would be getting a sister or brother. It was almost Christmas time. We had put up the tree. I had done all my shopping. We were baking cookies and singing Christmas carols.

I had a pain. I told Ron. I had another pain, and my water broke. I told him to call an ambulance. He took me for a joke. I called the ambulance. The ambulance came and he was still unbelieving. So they took me out, right past him on a stretcher to the ambulance.

The ambulance attendants wanted me to go to another hospital since we had to pass several hospitals. They thought I should go to one of those instead of Hartford Hospital. They didn't think I was going to make it that far. They did not want to deliver my baby.

We made it to Hartford Hospital. They ran with my stretcher in the doorway of emergency.

Tell was born December 20, 1974, seven pounds and fourteen ounces.

She was born while Ron was bringing the other children to my mom's house. He arrived right after I came out of the delivery room. He had seen the baby and was flabbergasted. He was happy though. She was beautiful.

I was allowed to go home two days later for Christmas Eve with my new baby. Ron picked me up. We picked up the other kids after showing my mom, stepdad, and siblings our new offspring.

Trev immediately claimed her as his baby. Wonie was mostly glad that her mother was on her way back home new baby or not.

We had a very nice Christmas.

I had built up enough time with my job, so I took my six weeks off to get us in order. It was nice to have a new baby in the house. Everyone helped me.

We had a house full of love, a new baby, and a dog.

Trev walked the dog without anyone asking him to. He was becoming very self-sufficient and a great helper.

CHAPTER 40

I went back to work finally. I was grateful for the sitter taking care of two of my children. She could also take care of Tell. She took care of newborns. She was able to do this while the other children were at school. She could give the babies her full attention. She would put them down for naps while the others were about to arrive from school. She was phenomenal. I was fortunately grateful.

Tell was trained and walking at ten months just like my other two children were. She had also sat in the bathroom with me in the mornings on her potty-chair. The first time I put ruffled panties on her she was through. She wouldn't dare go to the bathroom in them. If she had an accident, she cried because she messed them up. Tell was trained. Therefore, the sitter charged me less money to take care of her. Whoopee.

My children were still doing well with their school classes. Their health was great. Wonie was now only seeing the heart doctor once a year. Trev was running like he never had anything wrong with his ankles. However, my children had to fight often for one reason or another.

My eldest children were now big enough to go to the store for me. They always fought coming or going to the store. They always brought back from the store what they went to get though. Trev would also wait for Wonie to get out of school. She could also take care of him. She reminded me of me but, I never told her that.

I had just gotten back to my regular workload schedule. Now, Trev's teacher called me at work. She wanted to see me for a meeting. We set up an appropriate appointment time. I took the time off my job to go to the school. The teacher then told me that every day, about the same time, Trev falls out of his chair. He is distracting the other students in class. I asked her what the class was supposed to be doing at that time. She says they are having a rest period. I told her that he rests at home. He does not need to rest in school. I told her to give him something to do while the rest of the class rests. I told her that he falls because he is bored.

She didn't have that problem anymore.

Herb came to get the kids off and on. When it is off they get dressed. Trev is allowed to sit out on the stoop to await his father's arrival. Now, Wonie is a little tomboyish. So if she is allowed to go outside while she waits. By the time she is ready to go, her tights are dirty. So you may as well have a second pair handy if she was allowed to wait outside. So they waited and waited for a no-show.

So I deal with the attitudes like it is my fault that their father is irresponsible.

Last time it was on, he came and got them as scheduled. Yet upon his return with them, he complained that Trev liked to throw rocks and ran too much.

Duh, doesn't all normal little boys?

So they seldom see him for one reason or another.

CHAPTER 41

The children are still growing up in leaps and bounds. There was never a dull moment with three children.

I told my children to always bring their bikes through the living room and out of the back door. One day, I am cooking spaghetti and sauce. Trev came through the kitchen with his bike. He knocked over the sauce onto his side. He tried to catch it with his arm, but he got burned in both places. I took him to the hospital.

It must have been the day after Thanksgiving when I took leftovers out of the refrigerator. As I emptied the dishes into pots, Wonie washed them. I looked for my turkey dressing. I couldn't find it. She had thrown it down the garbage disposal. I tried to take my belt off to whip her. The part of the belt that goes into the belt hole came off and struck her in the temple. We went to the hospital.

The people at the hospital questioned my children and me. They threatened to take them away for child abuse. They found it funny when I said I was the one being abused. They sent them home with me.

Ron purchases us a fourteen-foot fiberglass-bottomed boat. He parked it in our front yard. It is just far enough over to the side for me to hang clothing on the clothesline. We go fishing most weekends. Everyone in the family can fish. Tell hands me the worms with gloves on. We all clean the fish we catch. I cook the fish for us.

Now outside the back door, there was a baseball diamond. The kids are allowed to play ball there. They usually have a large group of players. So one particular evening after dinner, they took Tell outside with them. They are responsible for watching her when she is allowed to go outside. Not too long after the game was started, I heard her screaming at the door. I opened the door to see my baby has an egg-sized swelling in the middle of her forehead. Trev and Wonie were standing behind her. They were both talking at the same time. I knew they were guilty. It was at least one of them. They never got their stories together. I whipped them both. I sent them to bed without a bath, after I had to sit Tell down with ice on her forehead.

This meant they would have to get up earlier in the morning to take showers before getting ready for breakfast and school.

Just a few days later, someone knocked on my door. It was a lady from across the street. This time Trev had thrown a rock across the street. The rock broke her window and struck her son. The rock had injured her son badly. She had taken her son to the emergency room. I ended up having to pay the bill for the window. I also paid for the stitches he had received.

CHAPTER 42

My children, being male and female, started to feel as though they should not be sharing a room together. One of them kept ending up in the bathroom to dress. They complained about it frequently. Therefore, our apartment started to feel cramped. They were growing so fast and crowding one another. Tell was ready to come out of the crib as well.

We also had a dog and a boat.

Ron and I started talking about the situation. We decided it was time to look for another apartment. Ron suggested that with both of us working, we should be able to buy a house. As a veteran, he should be able to purchase a house through the Department of Veteran's Affairs.

I was surprised with the prospect of buying a house. I didn't answer him right away. He kept bringing it up. So I gave it some real thought as to whether I wanted to live with a man like him. We thrived in this apartment, but to buy a house was like a permanent fixture. Then I said to myself, *What the heck.*

Mariea discussed it with her mother and her father. They both had met Ron and they both approved of the idea of them buying a house together.

I finally let him know that I agreed with him. We had been living together now for some years. It was working out okay. He paid half the household bills without me asking. He would want to know what the monthly budget was. He would break it up by the week. He would give it to me weekly without me asking for it.

So we started looking for a house. We looked at several houses. We found one on Sunset Street in Windsor. It had three bedrooms, a living room, a full basement, a front enclosed porch, a den with a fireplace, a garage, and a nice big yard. This was a beautiful house. The kids were running around in the yard like they already lived there. I was looking at the space. The kids could have their own rooms. The girls could share a room. The girls could have the bunk beds. I would buy Trev a new bed. The kitchen was big with a pantry. I was trying to stay calm.

He let me browse through it as long as I wanted to. Once he found out that I loved it. I was very pleased with it and I finally told him so. We gathered the kids up and we left the house. The kids were very excited. They were asking all kinds of questions. We talked about it a little. We then brought the kids to my mom. We told her about the house. She was happy for us. We left the kids with her.

We went to the agency and applied for the house that day.

By the grace of God, we got that house. Oh, my God, and all his goodness.

CHAPTER 43

We moved into this new house which was on the borderline of Hartford and Windsor. Sunset Street was a dead-end street. There were many houses up and down the street. There was a church at the top of the street on one corner of Main Street. There was a gas station on the other corner at the top of the street. We would live in the first house behind the gas station. There were railroad tracks down at the end of the street.

We went shopping for stove, refrigerator, living room furniture, den furniture, and a new bed for Trev. Wonie would keep the bunk beds. I had a washing machine, so we bought a dryer. I bought house and porch plants. We had thriving plants all over the place.

I registered Tell in the elementary school in Windsor. Both of my other children were registered at Seckman Catholic Junior High School through Project Concern. The two eldest children were going to be bused to school. Wonie loved it as she played on the basketball team and ran track. Trev didn't like it as much.

They soon got used to living in this new house. They were settling down in their schools.

We were sitting out front one afternoon. The kids were playing in the front of the house. Wonie saw a dog down the street that she thought was ours. She proceeded to go down to approach it. She got close enough to see that it was not ours. She turned and started to run with the dog on her tail. I was afraid for her but I knew not what to do. She got close to the house with the dog close to her. She proceeded to jump over a Volkswagen car. She cleared the car. The dog stopped running. He looked like, "What just happened?"

He turned and ran back down the street. I stood in amazement looking at my child, wondering how she could do that. I guess it must have been from her track training at school.

Trev didn't do so well in Catholic school. He soon had to get reregistered into Windsor Junior High School. He was able to get to play basketball with the team. He was really good at it. We went to most of his games. He would get high scores in all the games. I was excited watching him play after he had totally recovered from his ankles issues. I was more excited that he seemed to be settling down in this school. His grades proved some of that.

My job had recently moved to Windsor, so this was another convenience.

I thought now that I was in heaven. I had a house, a man, and my children were doing fantastic.

We settled into a routine of work, play, and keeping this house up. The kids now had chores. Trev would get up early to shovel snow from in front of the house and down the driveway before he went to school. Wonie did the dishes most nights. Trev dried the dishes and put them up. Ron would check the dishes. If he found one not to be clean, he would pile the sink back up. They would have to wash them again. They both started doing their own laundry and ironing.

School was great for them so they did their homework. When they did their homework, I checked it.

We went to drive-in movies. The family went to my dance shows.

We now had two dogs and a cat. Trev still walked the dogs as well. We bred Dobermans and the cat had many litters. We sold kittens and dogs.

Ron asked if he could bring his son Lonny to live with us because his mother was not raising him properly. I said yes. So he and Trev shared his room.

I was trying to correct Lonny's homework one night. I found out that he could not read well. I made the school keep him back a year for remedial teaching. He was mad, but learned to read that year. His sisters taught him how to clean a bathroom properly. He was now growing up in a normal environment.

His aunt decided that he should live with her at the end of that next school year.

We all got along very well while getting used to our own space.

CHAPTER 44

The children were really growing like weeds and doing crazy stuff still.

Trev was six-foot-four-inches at the age of thirteen. Wonie was short, maybe four feet ten inches. Lonny was short as well.

I would tell Trev to wear a certain pair of pants. He would tell me that they don't fit. These were new pants that I am talking about. I would make him put them on and come to let me see them. Sure as he had said, they were up around his ankles with the tags still on them. His foot size was also multiplying in size.

My children always had company. Now one of my friends, the one whose house I was abused in, she had two children a male and female. They were first cousins of my children. So they spent nights at my house frequently. Summer came and they all went to work on tobacco. The girls worked together. So did the male cousin and Trev work together on the same farm.

Wonie did very well. Trev started to have short paychecks. I later found out he and his cousin never worked all day. So he was short on cash when it came time to purchase school clothing. Trev had even less money as well, because both of my children had to give one-third of their paycheck to the household, one-third in the bank, and one-third in their pockets. So he was short all the way around.

Wonie stole a sex book from the bookmobile. She was curious and didn't think they would let her check out with it. They came and told me. I questioned her. She confessed. I made her return it.

I purchased myself a bike. I soon learned that I had to teach myself to ride. I didn't know how. I never had a bike growing up. I had once worked and purchased my siblings a bike for Christmas. They shared very well, but I never rode it. I now rode often. I got a little better, but traffic still scared me.

Trev stole my bike and went to Walmart to steal candy. I found out that this was not the first time. He got caught stealing this time.

He went to juvenile. I had to go rescue him. My bike got stolen during this episode. So I had not much time for my bike riding year. He was held until I went to get him. They didn't charge him. They just threatened him.

Wonie's female cousin spent the night. The next morning, she was missing a shoe. I couldn't imagine what happened to it. I found out when I left the house. I saw the footprints on the house. We had not too long ago painted it. The footprints were leading up to Wonie's window. The two of them confessed to leaving the house that night. They said they were so busy trying to get back to the house. That she had ran out of her shoe. I sent her home and told her to tell it to her mother.

One day after I left to go to work, Wonie and Trev broke my coffeepot. They took money out of my penny jar. They took their bikes and went to the store before they went to school. They replaced the coffeepot. When I arrived home from work, I needed to know why my coffeepot would not fit on the coffee maker. They would never tell on each other. So they most always both got the beating.

One day, my children decided to play on the railroad tracks. I had told them never to go down there. A train was approaching. They called to my baby who was not as fast as them getting off the track. They hollered at her to lay down between the tracks. They hollered at her to stay down. They kept hollering. That train ran over my baby, but she stayed down between the tracks.

It took me years to find this info out, and I am still mad at them.

Wonie smoked in the basement and threw her cigarettes by the furnace, but it was not her, she always said.

My children kept my life full of adventure. They stayed in stuff.

CHAPTER 45

Things in my life started to change again. Ron would have company over to play chess, smoke, and drink. This would be mostly when the kids were at my mother's. I learned how to play chess. I would beat his friends most of the time when they allowed me to play.

Ron and I started to go our separate ways more often than not now. My kids now had their own friends and were often not at home. Like now. We argued a lot. He would tell me that I should send my kids to live with their father. I would imply that he can't even come get them to visit. So why would I send them to live with him?

My children were home for one of these arguments. They wanted to know why he would say such things. I sent them to the playroom in Windsor that also had a swimming pool that day.

Wonie got into a fight at the center that day with a girl who liked Trev. He didn't give her the time of day. She took it out on Wonie. They came home and told me about it.

I later found out that Mr. B, the father of the girl that Wonie had fought with, was on the city council in Windsor. Mr. B came to my house that evening. We talked about the fight and he was not pleased with my comments. His daughter had gotten beaten very badly by my daughter. Even though Wonie had a scar in her face from it, the girl was showing off to her friends. She asked my children to leave and when they did not. She hit Wonie. Trev watched to make sure none of her friends jumped into the fight. He did not touch her. Someone broke the fight up. They were all asked to leave the center. My kids came home.

I refused to pay her emergency room charge. She started the fight and got beaten up.

He left my house still very angry.

CHAPTER 46

My relationship with Ron was now into its eleventh year.

My children are now in Catholic high school and Windsor High School, ninth and tenth grades. They like high school. Wonie enjoyed Catholic school. She played the clarinet. She was still running track and played basketball.

Our family went to one of Wonie's basketball games. She played well. She was fast. On this occasion, she rebounded by intercepting the ball. She ran up the court and made the shoot. She made the shoot in the other team's basket. She was running faster than she was thinking. She scored for the other team.

Trev is now playing on the Windsor High School basketball team. Tell is doing well in the elementary school. Trev and Wonie helped her with the metric system because I never learned it.

I am somewhat discontented. Ron and I are pretty much just going through the motions now. We don't agree on much. The bills get paid, but we are growing apart from each other.

I think one of our dogs, Kelly (the male), sensed my moods. When Ron is not at home, the dog comes into my room and puts his head on my bed by my feet. It's like he was saying, "I will protect you." I rubbed him, talked to him, got up, put him out, and closed the door.

Ron very often stays out late now on work nights. This is not the norm. It hasn't always been like this. We don't discuss it.

Ron started to take Tell over his grandmother's regularly. I didn't mind. I liked Gram. However, I dropped by one afternoon, and he wasn't there. He was surprised when he returned and I was there. I guess he had seen the car but still questioned why I was there.

I asked, "Is there a problem with me visiting Gram?"

He replied, "No, but why today?"

I said, "I had nothing else to do."

He let the discussion go.

CHAPTER 47

The school year came to an end. All my children passed to the next grade.

Wonie went back to work on tobacco. She now did piecework and made as much money as the other grown woman. She bought her own clothing and she saved money in her bank account.

Trev did not go back to tobacco. He went to work with one of my uncles, Dav. He was a window washer. He hired Trev to hold his ladder and help carry his equipment. He paid him very well. Trev was bored. I suggested he go back to tobacco and he said, "No, I'll work with uncle Dav." That's what I thought so he would say.

Trev was now managing his money better. Trev would say he needed sneakers. He would ask if he could go to New York to purchase some. The sneakers in Hartford were not his size. They only went up to size 11, and he wore size 12 now. They had bigger sizes and choices in New York. He would always have half of the money for his sneakers and his bus fare. How could I say no?

One particular day, Trev went to work as usual with his uncle. He was home from work early. He called me at my job. He stated that his uncle fired him. He got fired because he was on break and in the bar looking at TV. I had no sympathy. He knew his uncle was religious. He made a few calls, and by the time I came in from work, he had a job. This job was with another of his uncles, Wil. He went to work the next day and was pleased with the job. They did yard work and gardening. He paid well also. Trev worked the whole summer with him. He then had enough money to buy his school clothes that year.

Later that year, after the summer was over, Uncle Wil got his hand cut off in one of his electric yard tools. He went to the hospital. He stayed there for a while. We visited him in the hospital. We visited him when he went home from the hospital. He didn't like just being at home. He didn't like just lying around. He couldn't work yet. He died shortly after.

CHAPTER 48

The summer was coming to an end. I took the children to New York for school shopping. We stopped at the last gas station on the highway before getting to New York. We had to use the bathroom before we got to the city where they were few and far between.

We arrived on Jamaica Avenue in New York for them to shop. I dropped them off. They were supposed to meet me in two hours.

When I picked them up, I noticed that Wonie did an awful lot of shopping. I questioned her about it. She said she found good sales. I later found out that when we went to the gas station on the way there. We went to the bathroom. I was preoccupied with Tell. When Wonie went in the cash register had been open. She had robbed the gas station. She had given Trev some of the money so he wouldn't tell me.

It was not known by me then that I had driven the getaway car.

We visited my dad and stayed until late in the evening. We ate late and left. They slept most of the way home. We arrived home safely. The kids tried on and put their new clothing up.

I opened my mail. I received a letter telling me that the City Counsel of Windsor was going to bring some issues up for a vote. These issues would be discussed at a town hall meeting to be held in October. The issues decided on at the meeting would be brought up for a vote in November. One of the issues was redistricting. I would go to this meeting. I put the mail up, and I went to bed.

CHAPTER 49

My children started school in September in their new clothes with much pride. They had purchased them with their own money and their own styles.

Tell got accepted to a West Hartford Elementary School through Project Concern. My baby is now being bused to school like Wonie. She was well aware that she was going uptown to Duffy School in West Hartford. I knew what and where she was going. I knew what she would be up against, but she didn't.

She went to school on the first day on the bus for the first time. The bus ride was okay with her. However, she was a little upset about the new school. There were not many children there who looked like her just the ones who rode the bus with her. She had been one of the majority in her other schools. Now she was the minority.

I had a long talk with her about being black, beautiful, and female. I told her that the world was full of different kinds of people, of all kinds of colors. I told her that she was at that school for a better education. I told her not to worry about anything except how they treated her. If they treated her different from how they treated the others, then she was to tell me. I told her to tell me if they made her feel different. She was to tell me anything that made her feel uncomfortable. I told her that she was smart. I kept telling her that she should get all they had to give to her. That is if it was pertaining to her educational learning. I knew that their standards were higher than what she was used to. I also knew she was up to the task.

She followed my lead and we talked about it every day. She was doing okay so far. The things they taught her made her work hard and test her brain to keep up. She was aware of her surroundings, but in tune with the curriculum. She was proud to be smart. They called on her often to answer questions. She would come home and say they asked me this or that today. Mom, I knew the correct answer every time. She loved learning and the opportunity to prove it.

I wasn't worried about her. I was worried about them. I stayed on top of the situation. Her education meant too much to me.

She liked the bus ride even more now. She didn't have many problems. So we got used to her being there. She was moving right along in all areas.

CHAPTER 50

The day came for the town hall meeting. Ron didn't think it was necessary for him to attend. I didn't comment on that. I arrived about fifteen minutes early to the meeting. There were only a few people there when I arrived. I found a seat in the middle of the room and sat down.

The room soon started to fill up. The board members filed in. They took their seats. I immediately noticed Mr. B, the man whose daughter Wonie had fought with. This was the man who had left my house angry. Mr. B was one of the board members for the town of Windsor. I was surprised.

The meeting was called to order. They discussed the agenda. Then they finally got to the portion pertaining to the redistricting of the town lines of Windsor. There were only two streets that this discussion affected. I lived on one of them. My side of the street was in Windsor. The other side of the street, across the street from me was in Hartford. Next to those two streets were gas stations and a hotel. There were no residential properties after those two streets. So they wanted to draw Windsor town line after those two streets. They discussed this back and forth. The final vote on all the issues would be cast in November.

I discussed this with Ron. He could not be any more concerned. There was nothing he could do if they decided to draw their lines differently than they already had drawn them. I informed him that it would make a difference in the house taxes we paid. He could care less.

"You pay what they charge," he said.

Oh well, I would wait for the decision in November.

CHAPTER 51

The weekend came. Friends of ours were having a party. We usually attend their parties. They had invited us to this one. I questioned Ron about our attendance. Ron decided that he didn't want to attend. This was a Friday night. We didn't have any other plans. So I got dressed, took the kids to my mom's, and went alone. I had a wonderful time. I had such a good time that I didn't leave their house until the sun was coming up.

The sun was all the way up when I arrived at my house. I parked in the driveway and proceeded to enter the house. The door was unlocked. So I just dropped my keys back into my purse thinking nothing of it. I proceeded to go up the two stairs into the kitchen.

Ron was standing in the middle of the floor with a look that was way past angry on his face. He started shouting and cursing.

"Do you know what f——ing time it is?"

I said, "I don't have a curfew. I am more than grown." I said, "The party was nice. You should have went."

I proceeded to drop my purse on the table. I started to go into the bedroom. He blocked my path. When I tried to go around him, he punched me in the face. This punch knocked me off my feet. I fell and hit my head on the washing machine. I then laid on the floor for just a minute. I didn't want to fight a man again at this stage in my life. I thought I had left that mess behind me. I thought I had come too far away from that. No more abuse. I have had enough in this short lifetime.

In that minute, I had decided to just leave. I got up. We were face to face. I was hurting. He was still saying something.

I said, "You hit me for the first and last time."

He said, "Oh yeah."

He raised his hand to hit me again. I punched him in the stomach. He bent over. I snatched my purse off the table. I tried to run out the door. He grabbed at me. That turned into a shove down those two stairs to my back door.

I ran to my car. I got in before he could catch me. He came out of the house behind me. I backed out of the driveway and flew up the street.

CHAPTER 52

I had no idea where I was going. I pulled over and wept. I knew that I could not go to my moms and pick up the kids right then. I went to my sister's. I told her what happened. I told her that I didn't want to go back to that, nor did I want to go to mom's. I explained to her that I thought that once they start hitting you it doesn't stop. I learned that from lifelong experiences.

She understood because she had been there and almost still living in that same situation if not worst. Her kid's father, a heroin addict, had hit her in the head with a sixteen-ounce Pepsi-Cola bottle, and she is still with him. He is in jail right now.

So she understood abuse maybe.

She said I could stay with her and her four kids until her man got out of jail. I called my mom and explained to her the circumstances. I informed her that I would come get the kids later on in the afternoon. Once I could think straight. She was sympathetic, but understanding. She said okay.

I called Ron later that day after I had got some rest. He was trying to apologize. I explained to him that I was done. I told him that I wanted to come get some of my stuff. I would get the rest later. He didn't want it to be like that, but he said okay.

I finally went to bed with ice on my face. I went to sleep for a few hours. I awoke to my face looking almost normal. I went to the house. Ron kept trying to convince me that he was sorry. I accepted his apology. I still proceeded to gather up some of our stuff we would need them for the week. I left it like that.

I went to pick up the kids from my mom's. I talked to them about our circumstances. Tell cried for not being able to go home to her daddy. We went to my sisters and found room for our stuff and us.

CHAPTER 53

I missed going to work on that Monday. I had to find new bus stops for my girls, but Trev found his way to school.

I found out where my girls would catch their buses. So I went to work on Tuesday.

I talked to Ron and he decided to sell the house. I would take a five-thousand-dollar buyout. I told him when I would move my things out. I would put them in storage. I moved my stuff out by the end of the week. I did put them into storage the following Saturday.

I picked up my mail while I was there. I found out that the vote on redistricting had been taken. Our house on Sunset Street was now in the Hartford school district. I was no longer there. Trev was going to have to transfer from Windsor to Hartford school district. The girls were still in Catholic schools. Therefore, that decision did not affect them. Trev would be allowed to continue to go to Windsor High until the semester was over. This meant that after Christmas was over, he would have to transfer to Hartford schools for the third semester of the school year.

I took care of that transfer and discussed it with him. He was upset that he would be going to Hartford High School, but he accepted the fact. He had friends there.

The holidays passed. My sister and I cooked Thanksgiving dinner. We invited my mom, stepdad, brother, and adopted brothers over. They were all pleased. Christmas came and went. I bought my children what they needed. They understood that what we needed the most was an apartment. I needed to save my money for that.

I worked seven to seven most days. I was paying rent for living at my sisters. I was not spending much and banking more. I was trying to prepare by saving for us to get an apartment.

Sometimes, my sister's kids couldn't wait for me to get home from work to eat. They would fall asleep before I arrived, not eating supper. Not my cross to bear. They usually waited for me to cook when I got home. My sister didn't cook much now. My kids got used to me feeding them when I got there. So they did their homework while waiting for me. I fed them when I arrived. I checked homework. I would get clothing ready for the next day. We then bathed and slept. Things seemed to be moving in the right direction.

No matter what they still had me. I was thinking straight about their well-being.

CHAPTER 54

My job at the Hartford Insurance gave me a promotion. Therefore, I made more money in the midst of my craziness called life.

I got Trev situated in the Hartford High School system. Trev was playing basketball at Hartford High. One day while he was riding home with a coach, the coach decided to reach over and put his hand on Trev's thigh. At the next light, Trev got out of his car, found a phone booth, and called me.

I had told all my children about my molestation. I told them about people who take advantage of other people. I told them if they ever felt like someone was trying to take advantage of them not to hesitate to tell me.

I went and picked him up.

He was not doing well at Hartford High. His grades were As and Bs, but he fought. We had several school meetings about this. This latest meeting was at the board of education. I think Principal Cruz staged it that way to get rid of Trev. He had compiled the evidence against him. The people at the board of education suspended him. I was very upset.

I took him to Weaver High School and registered him for school there. Wonie decided that she no longer wanted to go to Catholic school. We discussed it further and she decided to stay there a little while longer. Trev didn't fare so well at Weaver. The curriculum called for them to teach remedial courses. That was the conclusion my child came to. Several of his classes had to learn the metric system before they could teach some subjects. My children already knew their metrics systems.

He was bored with that, so he acted out, of course. Therefore, he still stayed in trouble with the school system.

CHAPTER 55

The plot continued to thicken. I came home to my sister's house on a Friday evening. My sister wanted to talk to me. I paid her and we sat down. She informed me that she had just found out that day. So she informed me that her boyfriend was to get out of jail on that next Thursday. So I had to move out by then. She said she was sorry for the short notice.

I said, "Okay, no problem." I had the weekend to find an apartment or to miss work on Monday. *I could always go back to my mother's apartment*, I thought. *Yeah right*. I went to bed.

I got up on Saturday morning. My sister was apologizing repeatedly. I said that I understood. I fed the children and took them to my mother's house. I explained to my mother what the deal was. She offered me a room in her house if I couldn't find anything in time. I said thanks and left.

I got a newspaper. I set out on my new adventure. I checked out a few places to no avail. I finally found an "apartment for rent" sign on a building. It was an apartment building on the corner of Woodland Street and Albany Avenue. I called the number on the sign. The landlord met me at the apartment. He showed it to me. It was a one-bedroom apartment on the second floor. I looked at it and decided that it could work. So I lied and said that I only had one child. He rented the apartment to me. I signed the rental agreement. I paid him the rent. He gave me the keys. He said that I could move in immediately.

I picked up the kids and explained to my mom what I had done. She laughed and said, "By any means necessary."

I then went back to my sister's house. I talked to the kids about what I had gotten for us. They didn't care. They said at least it will be for us and us alone. We packed up our things that night. I left the food items. I called a few of my male friends to see if they could help me on Sunday. They agreed to do so. We slept at my sister's that night all ready for tomorrow.

On Sunday morning, I loaded up the car after breakfast. I removed all our belongings from her house. I put them into my car. I took them over to our new apartment. We parked in the back of the apartment where my parking space was located. We unpacked the car. We entered into our apartment with our things. The kids said it was okay. They were happy. It was nothing like the house we had left. However, it was ours. I took the kids back to my mom's.

I proceeded to rent a U-Haul truck. I picked up a few fellows who said they would help me. We went to the storage. I got what I needed from there. I purchased a couch that would open up into a bed. We went to the apartment. We parked the truck in the back where I would later park my car since my car was at the U-Haul office. We unloaded the truck. They tried to ask me what happened. I just said it wasn't working out after eleven years. We returned the truck. I paid them for their help. I dropped them off.

I went and picked up some groceries for the week. I went to get my children. We then went to our new home. I parked in the back-yard. We all went up the back stairs. I opened the door and they were at home and happy to be there.

CHAPTER 56

I put my big kids in the bedroom with their bunk beds. I made a bed out of the let-out couch in the other room. This was the living room by day and a bedroom by night for Tell and I. I cooked us dinner in our new apartment. We all got ready for Monday morning. Tell slept while I tried to watch TV.

I missed going to work that Monday morning on time. I made sure my children got to their bus stops on the corner of Albany Avenue. I got bus schedules. Trev could walk to school. I rode him this morning. I had to go by his school to get to work late anyways.

My children were waiting for me outside the apartment building when I got home from work. I immediately went and got keys made for them and an extra for me. I had forgotten to do that yesterday. We settled in and watched a little TV before bedtime.

The children got used to living there, so they would go visit friends and come back before too late. I worried about them being out on the corner of Albany Avenue at night. They seemed to be doing all right in school. I wasn't so sure. After a few weeks, Wonie started complaining about the Catholic school again.

I transferred her to Weaver as well. She didn't find the school-work hard at all. She skipped classes and school a lot at times. She kept her grades up though.

It must have been about a month later. I was at work and received a phone call from the police department to pick Wonie up. It was apparent to them that she and a friend were in this ladies' house with her man. The lady called the police on them and detained them until the police arrived. She decided not to press charges since her man had to have let them in. It was obvious. The man was in the house and the house was not broken into. Wonie blamed her being there on the other girl. She was just going there with her friend, she said. I punished her. I told her to go to school from now on. I told her to stay away from these men. I told her to stay out of their houses with or without her friends.

Within the next two weeks, the school called me at work to pick Trev up from school. Apparently, there was a food fight in the cafeteria. The whole lunchroom was a mess. However, they blamed it all on Trev. They said he started it. They suspended him and needed to turn him over to his parent.

CHAPTER 57

Ron visited us. During his visit, he stated that I couldn't possibly be happier where I was living than I was at the house we shared. I didn't comment. I had peace of mind. I thought about that. The kids were wilding and it showed. Wonie was hanging out with hoodlums on Albany Avenue. Trev never had acted out quite so much in school as he was now.

I decided that living in this apartment was not going good for my children. So that statement made me rethink my objectives. I may have been losing my children while trying to keep a roof over their heads and working. I decided that I needed to move off the corner of Albany Avenue. I started my searching through newspapers and by word of mouth.

I found a new apartment. It was on Sargent Street. It was a first floor apartment in a six-apartment building. I called the landlord. I set up an appointment to see it. We met and he showed me the apartment. It had three bedrooms, a large kitchen, and plenty of space. It was also roach-infested.

I made a deal with him that if I took it he would have to pay for the supplies I would need to get rid of the roaches. He agreed. I took it in the middle of the month in spite of the rodents. He deducted a hundred dollars from my security deposit for my supplies. I bombed the apartment every other day in every room until the first of the month came. By the first of the month, I had run the roaches to the other parts of the building. I went with supplies again. I did not see any roaches on two occasions.

My rent was paid in the other apartment where I was living until the first of the month. So I didn't have to rush to pack my things. I had the time I needed to set up my plan to move. I told the kids about our new apartment. They were glad that we would again have some much-needed space.

By the first of the month, I had cleaned out the apartment we were in. I was ready to take my things out of storage. I purchased myself a rocking chair to go with the let-out couch. I had left Ron the living room set to sleep on when I left the house. I took my bedroom set and other things out of storage. We moved into our latest apartment.

CHAPTER 58

Once I had secured this new apartment, I had registered both Trev and Wonie at Hartford High School. Wonie would be away from some of her Weaver friends. So she did well settling in. She has a photographic mind so she would do well with her subject matter.

I should say I reregistered Trev. They took him back reluctantly, because we lived in their school district. He would also do well for a while. He got back on the basketball team and excelled in his studies.

The apartment was okay. I still bombed it every weekend. I felt like the building was infested, but it wasn't going to affect me. The kids had their space again. They were happy about it. Once again, I found a bus stop for Tell's school bus. Wonie and Trev could walk to school.

I had reconnected with an old male friend and that was going good so far. I shortly found out that he already had a girlfriend. I also realized that he was using hard drugs. My friends were more than happy to tell me to check it out. I thanked them for that information. That was the beginning of the end of that relationship. I had no need for that situation. We remained friends but nothing more.

My children and I were beginning to really settle in and utilizing all our newfound freedom of space again. We all had enough space to breathe in now.

My kids and I were sitting in the kitchen one night after living at this apartment for a while. We heard a noise in my daughter's bedroom. The window had been opened for air circulation. Someone had just stepped on into the house through that window. Trev was the first to investigate the noise. It was some middle-aged man looking like he was homeless. Trev apprehended him with no problem. He then brought him into the kitchen by force. He was sat down at the table while I called the police.

Trev tried to scald him. I stopped him but not before he got to pour some hot water on the man. This man said he was looking for some fictitious-named person. We detained him until the police came. The policeman questioned us all. They then took that man away. We were somewhat in shock. We soon learned that we needed to secure this apartment which is what we did. However, we never opened our windows again. We got a lot of fans for that apartment.

CHAPTER 59

It seems like my children only gave me enough time to catch my breath before the next episode of our lives materialized.

Trev was not happy at Hartford High. Things for Trev at school were starting to escalate again. Not so much with students as it was with his teachers. I think having come from Weaver High School, he may have thought he knew more than they were trying to teach him. However, I was not ready for more drama.

I took the family to a cookout at a cousin's house in Bloomfield. It was great. It was sort of like a very much-needed escape from reality. Somehow, the subject came up about Trev and his many school problems. My cousin and I ended up discussing him living with her in her Bloomfield home. We would then try to get him into Bloomfield High School. We were in agreement on the subject since she was now living alone. Her kids had all moved out. He could be some company for her. She ended up writing me a letter to bring to the school.

That Monday, I took him with the letter to the school. I explained to them the situation. They accepted him. I was then able to transfer him from Hartford High School. I registered him into Bloomfield High School system that day.

I was somewhat relieved for the moment. He seemed to be doing very well in Bloomfield High School. He tried out and got to play on the basketball team. There were not many blacks on the team, but that didn't seem to matter to him. The Hartford High School team had also been diversified. He soon became one of the top scorers on the team. Our family went to most of the games. I was ecstatic with the prospect that maybe he had found his place in the school system. He did well in his subject matters. He was a B-plus student as well.

However, there was this young lady who liked him. He didn't pay her much of the attention she desired. So one day, she threatened him with the fact that he didn't belong there. She also said that his days were numbered.

He came home to my apartment that day. We discussed the issue. I told him to continue to ignore her if he was not interested in her like that. I was surprised that he brought this home to me.

Since he and I both knew he was a womanizer.

CHAPTER 60

I awoke to a snowy day. The girls bundled up, but they didn't mind going to school in the snow. I left for work. It was a very snowy, breezy day today. It seemed almost like we were having a blizzard. My visibility was very bad. I was driving to work very slowly. It didn't matter much what time I got there. I had given myself some extra time. In this kind of weather conditions, they would not mind what time I arrived as long as I came.

I was about a block away from my job now. I was approaching the corner to turn left. My job would then be straight up the road.

Then, just before I could make that left turn, I was hit by a fourteen-wheeler truck. My car was flipped onto its right side. I was hanging by the seat belt. I was totally dazed. The driver got out of the truck. He approached the car. He called out to me. He knocked on the window. I responded. He opened the door. He reached in and unleashed the seat belt. He held on to me to keep me from falling over. He then pulled me out of the car. He laid me on the ground while saying he was so sorry. He said that he did not see me. He called an ambulance after wrapping me in a blanket.

I hurt all over.

The ambulance came. I was wrapped in more blankets. I was taken to the hospital. They kept talking to me asking where I hurt. I remained in the hospital for three days. They tested my entire body. I had no broken bones. I had an achy body from the impact of being hit by the truck. They finally allowed me to go home. I had to go to my mothers. I still could not properly function. I was on the couch when I wasn't in the bed. I was weak and in a lot of pain. My daughters were already at my mom's house. Trev was still staying at my cousins in Bloomfield.

Thank God for my mother. She cooked for us. She supervised the girls. My siblings went to my apartment. They got what my girls needed to function while I couldn't help them. They brought the food items I requested. They were worried about me. They were glad to help because they had never seen me when I was not capable of managing.

CHAPTER 61

During this recuperation period of mine, Trev would visit. He would go to school, play ball, and come visit me every day. He was distraught. He would say I didn't look well. He would ask what the doctor was saying about my recovery. He would go back to my cousins and do the same things the next day.

He had worked his way up from the bottom on the basketball team. He had gotten two certificates for participation and honorable mention basketball. He was now playing on the varsity team. Before the accident, we had gone to one of his games where he scored twenty-eight points, thirteen points were in the third quarter. I was so proud of him.

One particular day, he was plumb worn-out when he came to visit me. We both fell asleep. He ended up spending the night. He went to school from my mother's in Bellevue Square to Bloomfield High School by bus in the morning.

Trev seemed to be doing well. However, that same young lady kept at him. She was still saying, "Count your days." This was all because he would not have anything to do with her. He talked to me about this again. This little white girl was becoming a pain in the neck. She seems not to be able to take his rejection.

CHAPTER 62

I started to feel like my old self slowly. I was beginning to do more than lay on the couch. I went to my doctor's appointment. It felt pretty good to be up and out again. It was three or four weeks before I was released to go back to work.

My car repairs were finally done. I picked my car up. I waited for my girls to come to my mom's house from school. I took my family back to our own apartment, with the exception of Trev. He still stays with my cousin in Bloomfield. I talked to him on the phone and he was glad that I was functioning again. I told him not to worry and to get some rest.

I had mended well. I returned to work where it seemed as though they had saved my work for me. There was surely not a shortage of work. I felt needed again. I got lost in the work and the days flew by.

I usually ate lunch alone in their shack. It was by their little lake in the back of the building. I would write down my thoughts during that time. It freed my mind.

One day, I wrote a poem. It is now in a book called *Forever and a Day*, published by the International Library of Poetry with 2,500 other poems.

Thoughts For My Day

I don't know what I'm feeling, confusions not the word. I'm kind of angry, hesitant to speak for fear of not being heard. The mix-up of my mind makes crossword for the blind. To decipher my thoughts, burn up every cross, would mean nothing to no one (Not true I now know). Alone, surrounded, but alone, insensitive to any and all. Why me? In awe, I wonder if maybe one day, probably a long, long time away. The pieces will fit, the weight should shift, peace, resignation set in, for me my life again.

To do what? With whom? where, how, not now. Then when will it be? If at all a life is meant for me. Existence is not substantial when anxieties are pointed in other directions. My physique is questioned by daily minute diversions of things I'd like, but can't be for me. Not now, I see. Will time frames make up for years untouched, of thoughts untold, of dreams to unfold? Who knows? Not me. I can't wait to see if I will achieve the ultimate me, or is this the way it was meant to be?

I wrote this while I ate lunch sitting out in the shack by the lake. I looked at it and said, "Wow."

It didn't free my mind today. It only made me think the rest of the afternoon. I thought about my life.

CHAPTER 63

The weather was starting to feel warm again. The season was starting to change. Spring was on the rise. I went to work and received a call from Tell's school. I needed to go in for a conference. I set it up for later in the week.

I arrived at Duffy School in West Hartford for the conference.

Tell, myself, and her teacher went into the conference room. We greeted each other, after our formalities. The teacher said that Tell called him out of his name. I couldn't understand that initially. She wasn't that kind of girl. Therefore, they wanted to know if I would allow them to do a mental analysis on her. This analysis would go into her school record. This analysis would follow her through her school years.

I wanted to know what brought this about. Well, it seems as though it was because she had called him G. I. Joe. Yep, she called him G. I. Joe. I nicely informed him that G. I. Joe was a good guy, so what was wrong with her calling him that?

I then stated that by no means, could they analyze my child. Nor could they put anything but her grades into any kind of file. I told him that especially not a special file to follow her through her school years.

They sent her home for two days. That was just fine with me. I took her home from that school right then.

CHAPTER 64

Tell went back to school after the two-day suspension. We had discussed the situation more than once. She listened to what I told her to do. She did her schoolwork. She hardly talked to that teacher unless he called on her in the classroom.

It was almost Easter. I had shopped with my children for their Easter clothing. We had bought our food for Easter dinner.

One of my girlfriend's mothers had bus trips to go to Riverside Park on Easter. So I had booked seats on their bus for my family. We would go to Riverside Park with them on the bus trip this year. This would be after we had gone to church. I had previously gone on this bus trip with them many times. That was before I had the children. It always made for a good Easter day at the park.

Easter arrived. We ate breakfast. We dressed and went to church. They looked and felt good in their new clothes. After church we ate some lunch and we went to catch the bus for Riverside Park.

We arrived at the Park. I bought tickets that allowed them to ride all the rides. They ran from ride to ride. They even rode some rides with Tell. It truly was a great day. The kids ate and rode on all the rides until it was time to leave. We all slept going home on the bus.

We arrived back in Hartford. I loaded them into the car. I dropped Trev at my cousin's house. We said our goodbyes. He went into the house. We proceeded to go to our house. We bathed and went to bed after a very lovely Easter day.

CHAPTER 65

I got up and fed the girls. We got dressed and set out for school and work.

I drove to work. When I arrived, it was April Fools' Day. So I played a trick on the other office workers.

We all laughed. They said that they owed me. We went to our desks. We all started to work, still laughing. I got busy at work as usual. I stayed on my ringing telephone. There seemed to be more issues today than on a usual Monday. I went to lunch. I then returned to my desk. I also returned to my ringing phone.

This phone call was different. It was from the Bloomfield Police Department. They asked to speak to me. I informed them that it was I whom they were speaking to. They told me that they had a warrant for my arrest. They said I could turn myself in or that they could come and get me. I asked them to allow me to finish my day at work. I would come in and surrender myself to them. They obliged me my wishes. They gave me until 6:00 p.m.

They thought that they were coming to burn a cross in my front yard. That was if I allowed them to come for me. That was if I allowed them to arrest me at my house. No way did I want my children to see me go to jail for anything.

I then received another call from the state senator, Frank Barrows. Mr. Barrows had knowledge of my impending arrest. He offered to go with me to the police department to turn myself in. He said that he would meet me there.

I was overjoyed.

CHAPTER 66

I tried to finish my work day. I didn't get much work done. My mind was consumed with the thought of going to jail.

I left work and went to the Bloomfield Police Department. I arrived at the police department. Mr. Barrows was already waiting for me. He introduced himself to me. We proceeded to go inside the police department together. I identified myself to the officer at the front desk. I surrender to the police. They talked a little to me about charges. I was then booked. I was fingerprinted. They took a mug shot. They then put me into a cell and slammed it shut. I sank down to a cot. My legs could no longer hold me.

I was booked and charged with first-degree larceny. This was on April 1, 1985. What an awful April Fools' Day joke to be played on me.

I was the *first* person ever to be arrested for stealing free public education. This was because Trev maintained a B average in Bloomfield High School. They could not take that away from him. So they arrested me for sending him to their school. Even though he stayed with my cousin in Bloomfield, he stayed at her address located in Bloomfield.

I could not understand their rationale. When they take my state taxes, they don't only use them for Hartford where I lived. They use them for the whole state of Connecticut.

I sat in jail for a few hours before being released. They released me on a promise to appear in court on April 8, 1985.

I thanked Senator Barrows. He informed me that he had a lawyer, Donald Cardwell, for me. I missed work the next day. I met with Don Cardwell on that day instead. We discussed this upcoming case. He would represent me in court. I have no idea who paid him. He said something about "pro bono." I did not know what that was. I did know that it wasn't being paid by me. At that first court appearance, they continued the case. The judge transferred my case to May 8, 1985, at the higher court—superior court.

CHAPTER 67

I had discussed this incident with my children. Trev was now at home in my apartment. I explained what it was about and why they arrested me to my children. During this discussion I found out that Trev had gotten wind of this before it happened. He didn't know what to do when he heard about it. He had dropped out of Bloomfield High School to try to keep it from happening. My baby boy had a heart for his mother.

He had found out that the girl who kept bothering him was the daughter of a bigwig in Bloomfield. The Bloomfield town hall had a meeting and decided that there were too many people going to their schools that didn't live in Bloomfield. They had videos. These were from their private eyes. They had videos of several of the children.

The committee had a video surveillance of Trev. This was when he had spent the night at my mother's. They taped him when he was leaving my mother's house. They taped him getting off the bus going to Bloomfield High School. This was during the time of my recovery from the accident. They stated that he lived at my mother's. This was not true, but I was now fighting their city hall in court.

Several others got arrested. Some were even arrested on the same day as I. However, I was still the first to be arrested for stealing free public education.

CHAPTER 68

I started making court appearances. They kept continuing the case. So we kept going to court. The newspapers started taking pictures of my coming and going to the court. They had a field day. We appeared as front page news all around the United States. We were also on the news every day. You couldn't turn on the news without hearing about our case. You couldn't pick up a newspaper without seeing our faces.

We were on the front page of *Wall Street Journal*. They stated that it was all about "economic disparity" and "equal education." Senator Barrows got cited by city hall for standing up with us for Equal Education everywhere.

I met with the Mayor Milner. Mayor Milner brought Jesse Jackson to town to meet with me. The mayor and Jesse Jackson took Trev and I to dinner to discuss the case.

We had two offers to do a movie about our lives. We had offers from Lorimar Productions and Universal Studios. I was baffled. I didn't know anything at that time except that Lorimar was the larger of the two. I chose Lorimar on that factor alone. What did I know?

They visited us at our home. They discussed the case. I signed a nondisclosure waiver. They gave us a founder's fee of five thousand dollars. That was to hold us while we waited for their final decision.

They ended up not doing the movie. It was political and Jesse Jackson couldn't get enough politicians to stand up for it with him.

I purchased us all new furniture. I was trying to make our lives as normal as possible. My children didn't know what to think. Neither did I. They were trying to figure out if I was going to do the twenty years that this case held or what. They didn't know if I was going to be found guilty or not. They didn't like the publicity. This life was not normal for us.

I kept working for a bit. It was very uncomfortable having people in my face about my issue. I then went back to the post office. I took the test again and scored high. I got the job. It was from 3:00

p.m. to 11:30 p.m. so it wouldn't interfere with my court dates. I couldn't get back the time I had worked for the post office before. I was going to start over again with a clean slate. No time served, but that was okay.

The case was finally dismissed. I got no time, but I still have the first-degree larceny charge on my record to prove that I was arrested and charged. That I went through the muck and the mire of it.

I gave my two weeks' notice to the Hartford Insurance Company, but I quit the next week.

CHAPTER 69

I tried to continue life as though nothing was happening outside my house. I moved to Love Lane. It was somewhat off the main drag. It was a three-bedroom apartment on the third floor. My children were happy with it.

Trev was back at Hartford High School in an alternate learning center in the eleventh grade.

Wonie was hanging in there in the twelfth grade. It was prom time for her and she didn't want to go. She didn't have an escort. Trev decided that he could take her. I agreed and paid for it. They went and had a good time.

Getting my children's education had taken its toll on me. It should not be this hard for a parent. I had stood up to the task, but it had beaten me down. Trev once again was not satisfied with the alternate learning center. We discussed it. Trev had a plan to propose to the school system. They agreed.

My son Trev then beat the normal school system. He doubled his English classes. He took eleventh-grade and twelfth-grade English.

He became a double promote. He aced them by passing them both. He then had enough credits. He had all the required subject matter taken care of.

Trev and Wonie graduated from Hartford High School together. Both of my children graduated the same year from Hartford High School. They really thought that they were twins then.

They went off to Bakersfield College in California and Miami-Dade College in Florida.

CHAPTER 70

Mariea was now content with herself and her achievements. She was still moving forward. She now has only one more child to get through school. She is still working. She felt good about her accomplishments this far, even though this life and many people have done wrong by her. She is now moving out of the limelight and farther into the shadows. She is at peace with herself and her surroundings.

She and Tell moved to Grafton Street into a two-bedroom apartment. They continued to live out their lives together. It was now just the two of them with the other two in college.

So now that the whole world knew that after all her life matters of living in heaven and hell, she persevered with her head held high. She was always trusting in the Lord.

Everyone everywhere knew that she got arrested and jailed on a first-degree larceny charge.

They all knew.

She was the first ever to be *arrested for stealing free public education*.

THE END

ABOUT THE AUTHOR

S. Aminiah Nialiah, also known as Saundra Mariea Foster.

Saundra was raised in the projects and streets of Hartford, Connecticut, and New York. Saundra is now a middle-aged woman whose life from the beginning was a steep uphill climb. She has privately been telling her stories through her many dance/drum worlds since her tender age of seven. On many stages, she told her many stories through interpretations of her body movements in tap shoes or bare feet. She rose to the occasions.

She has had many struggles through her life just trying to raise her three children and stay alive for them, most times, alone.

She strived to get a quality education for them. Those efforts caused her to have to give every bit of herself to their causes. She has now decided to share some of those stories with others.

She now resides in St. Louis, Missouri.

CPSIA information can be obtained
at www.ICGtesting.com
Printed in the USA
FFHW021418080819
54163711-59867FF